CARRIE

PRIDE
AND
JOY

Terri
Casey

PRIDE

AND

JOY

The Lives and Passions of
Women Without Children

TERRI CASEY

BEYOND
WORDS
Publishing
I N C

Beyond Words Publishing, Inc.
20827 N.W. Cornell Road, Suite 500
Hillsboro, Oregon 97124-9808
503-531-8700
1-800-284-9673

Editors: Phyllis Hatfield and Ann Granning Bennett
Design and typography: Susan Shankin
Proofreader: Joseph Siegel
Managing editor: Kathy Matthews

Printed in the United States of America
Distributed to the book trade by Publishers Group West

Library of Congress Cataloging-in-Publication Data

Casey, Terri.
    Pride and joy : the lives and passions of women without children /
Terri Casey.
        p.   cm.
    Includes bibliographical references.
    ISBN 1-885223-82-X
    1. Childlessness — United States — Case studies. 2. Women —
United States — Psychology. I. Title.
HQ535.C29   1998
305.4'0973 — dc21   98-7952
                                                               CIP

The corporate mission of Beyond Words Publishing, Inc.:
Inspire to Integrity

TO MY HUSBAND, DAVE HUSSEY

TO MY MOTHER, AGNES SAVASKY

CONTENTS

INTRODUCTION

We read books to find out who we are. What other people,

real or imaginary, do and think and feel is an essential guide to our

understanding of what we ourselves are and may become.

URSULA LeGUIN

"THEY'RE MY PRIDE AND JOY!" IT'S AN expression that mothers have used for decades to describe how they feel about their children. The women in this book, however, take pride and feel joy in their lives without having borne children. And they represent the increasing number of voluntarily childless women in our society.

Even though more women than ever before are choosing not to have children, it's not always easy for them to go against the pro-motherhood social, cultural, and familial conditioning they—and all of us—receive as children, teens, and adults. Libraries, bookstores, and supermarket checkout lines are full of books and magazines on mothering—how to prepare for it, the physical and emotional stages of it, the infinite aspects of it. Television sitcoms more often than not depict women as mothers, and most fictional characters in novels who start out as single or married working women without children usually come around to the "inevitable" place of wanting to have children. Motherhood continues to be portrayed as a woman's prescribed role.

I myself chose not to have children, and my life has been deliciously full with marriage, family and friends, work, play, travel, and education. Throughout the 1970s, when I was in my 20s, I watched many high school, college, and work friends get married and have babies. From time to time I noted my lack of interest in having children but was too active and happy for that to seem a problem. I was drawn to exploring other countries and cultures. I studied literature, cultivated friendships, enjoyed athletics and the outdoors, and began my journalism career as a correspondent for a medium-sized newspaper.

In 1987, when I was 33, my career took me from the newsroom to a software corporation where I wrote articles about the human side of the high-technology boom. During that time, another boom—a baby boom—was occurring all around me as one colleague after another announced she was pregnant, enjoyed her baby shower, and went on maternity leave. A few friends confided their struggles with infertility. Around the same time, the American political chant became "family values," implying that only married couples raising children were living decent lives worth emulating.

Amidst all this I continued to love my freedom to spend a lot of time with my husband, family members, friends, and by myself, to travel, write, change jobs, remodel an old house, volunteer for a variety of organizations—in short, to design the personal and professional life that suits my nature best. Yet I also noticed the subtle biases against and misconceptions about childless women evident in the remarks occasionally aimed at us. Over the years various neighbors, co-workers, well-intentioned acquaintances and even strangers have commented on my maturity, sexuality, and relationships with observations such as, *"When you finally settle down, you'll want to start having kids," "When a woman has a baby, she feels like a real woman,"* and *"The holidays must be such a sad time of year for you, without a family."* I came to see that women who choose not to become mothers are considered to possess particular character flaws: We are *self-centered, immature, workaholic, unfeminine, materialistic, cold, neurotic, child-hating.* I heard about mothers who were pained by their daughters' decisions not to follow in their steps, husbands who were confused by their wives' ambivalence about motherhood, siblings who froze every time the subject of babies came up in their childless sister's presence. I understood how, given stereotypical images and strained relationships, the many women today who are uncertain about motherhood may not easily embrace the option of a childfree life.

Just before I turned 40, I began to wonder how many women were childless by choice and what their lives were like. How did they spend the time and energy and money that women who are mothers typically spend on their children? What were their dreams for their future? Were they as happy as I am?

About four years ago I indulged that curiosity. I looked for summaries of research done on childlessness over the last 20 years or so, and I saw that many of the studies did not distinguish between the voluntary and involuntary states.[1] But the primary

---

[1] Those who did distinguish between the states used various terms to describe women who choose not to have children: childless-by-choice, voluntarily childless, childfree. Each of these words carries a slightly different nuance that's appropriate for or preferred by different women. But rather than be an arbiter of language, I, too, have used the terms interchangeably.

researchers—Jean Veevers of the University of Toronto in the 1970s, Sharon Houseknecht of Ohio State University in the 1980s, and a few others who more recently have built upon their pioneering work—created a revealing profile of childfree women that looks like this:

Women who choose not to have kids tend to be either "early articulators," who have a sense even as children or teenagers that they are not drawn to motherhood, or "postponers," who wait to decide about having children and find they have developed a lifestyle they love and don't want to give up. Childfree women tend to be firstborns or "only children" who are independent and high achievers. They're commonly well educated, hold high-status jobs, earn above-average salaries, and live in cities. Most of them are not affiliated with an organized religion—not surprising, since they're nontraditional in several areas of their lives and since many religions consider childbearing the purpose and duty of a married woman.

When researchers ask women who are intentionally childless why they chose not to be mothers, the women most often talk about wanting to be free—free to pursue self-development and self-fulfillment, free from childcare responsibilities, free to be spontaneous and mobile. They see their decision as natural and their lives as holding unlimited potential. Career is often mentioned as a reason why women forgo motherhood, as is the desire for a satisfying spousal relationship.[2] So are financial independence and concerns about overpopulation.

[2] Data shows that marital satisfaction is greater among childless couples, who tend to have more egalitarian relationships and spend more time together. Also that couples with children don't approach pre-baby levels of marital happiness until all of their children have left home. (Studies by the U.S. National Opinion Research Center covering data from 1973 to 1994, and by sociologist Mary Bennin of Arizona State University in 1997.)

How many women are choosing not to have children? In 1997 the U.S. Census Bureau study "Fertility of American Women" reported that while in 1976 only 35 percent of American women between the ages of 15 and 44 were childless, by 1996 the rate was 42 percent. The most dramatic increase was seen in women between ages 35 and 39: from 1976 to 1996 the percentage of women who didn't have children nearly doubled, from 10.5 percent to 19.7 percent. Given that the rate of childlessness is increasing faster than the rate of infertility, demographers theorize that more women are choosing not to have children. Amara Bachu, the statistician-demographer who headed the study, has said that she expects the average rate of childlessness could double in a decade, given women's increasing career opportunities, economic concerns, the infertility that can result from postponing childbearing, and the stress and worry that accompany raising children today.

Other sources also point to a trend in voluntary childlessness. The same year the U.S. Census Bureau study appeared, *American Demographics* magazine reported that while the rate of childlessness has not yet reached Depression or pre-World War II levels, it has steadily increased since the 1950s baby boom and today is up even from the early 1990s. Childless by Choice, an information clearing-house for people without children, says that even in the current baby boom, one in seven married couples of childbearing age in the United States is opting out of parenthood. Membership in organizations such as No Kidding! in Canada and the United States and the British Organisation of Nonparents is on the rise.

A similar trend shows up in Britain, Australia, New Zealand, and Japan. In Great Britain, a survey of 76,100 patient records published in the October 1993 *British Medical Journal* showed that one in ten women chose not to have children. In 1997 the Australian Bureau of Statistics reported in *Australian Social Trends* that families consisting of a married couple with no children increased from 30.3 percent of the population in 1986 to 33.9 percent in 1996. The University of Canterbury reports that in New Zealand in 1981 about 11 percent of 50-year-old women had no children, but by the year 2000 the figure is expected to reach about 20 percent, or one in five. And a poll commissioned in September 1997 by the prime minister of Japan showed that childless marriages are gaining greater acceptance among Japanese: of 3,574 adults aged 20 or older surveyed, almost half responded that having children is not important for married couples.

In researching this topic, I found that in the last few years major newspapers and magazines in the United States, Britain, Canada, and Australia have run articles related to voluntary childlessness. I also found several books on chosen childlessness published in the 1970s and early 1980s celebrating the expanded career opportunities and new freedom from gender-specific roles that women were enjoying at the time. A few more titles published in the late 1980s and first half of the 1990s offer new research and insights, and several authors provide personal accounts of prolonged and anxious ambivalence about motherhood. As I read these later books, I began to understand how long and hard some women suffer over whether or not to have children. Yet I also knew from my own and others' experiences that many women make their decision about this early in their lives and with confidence, and many who postpone the decision don't experience great angst when they eventually make it.

Although I found all of this information compelling, nowhere did I find what I most wanted to read: stories from a diverse cross section of women talking at length about their lives, decisions, and pursuits. I wanted to hear these stories from the original sources, and I set about finding women willing to speak out. Once I heard their stories, I realized that I wanted to pass them on.

In *Kitchen Table Wisdom: Stories That Heal,*[3] Rachel Naomi Remen, M.D. says, "All stories are full of bias and uniqueness; they mix fact with meaning. This is the root of their power. Stories allow us to see something familiar through new eyes. We become in that moment a guest in someone else's life, and together with them sit at the feet of their teacher. The meaning we may draw from someone else's story may be different from the meaning they themselves have drawn. No matter. Facts bring us to knowledge, but stories lead to wisdom." The power of stories—especially a collection of them—made me want to invite the women I found to tell their own.

In this book you'll find edited transcripts of my interviews with 25 women who are finding meaning, purpose, self-esteem, and security apart from motherhood. In reading their stories, women who have already decided not to have children will feel affirmed (even if they don't need validation). Women debating whether to have children might find their ambivalence reduced or resolved. Women who have struggled with infertility, and women with mates who don't want children—or want no more children—might find comfort and encouragement. Family and friends of women who don't care to be mothers might gain information and understanding.

The women I interviewed range in age from 25-year-old Maria Rodriguez to 84-year-old Ruby Burton. Why include the young, when there's so much time for them to change their minds? Why include the old, when most women interested in this question are under age 50? This is why: Many of the middle-aged and older women in the book say they knew their minds early when it came to not wanting to have kids, and that validates the younger voices. What's more, women in their 20s and 30s who are pursuing a career

---

[3] *Kitchen Table Wisdom: Stories That Heal,* by Rachel Naomi Remen, M.D. (New York: Riverhead Books, 1996).

are questioning whether they can "have it all," and their peers in this book might help shed light on that issue. Conversely, a question that women of any age who choose to be childless hear frequently is, "Who will take care of you when you're old?" The answers that childless elders offer might help allay that fear.

The narrators of these stories form a diverse group. They are married, partnered, cohabiting, single, divorced, and widowed, from privileged backgrounds and disadvantaged ones, happy families and troubled ones. They are of varied ethnicities and cultural traditions, and they grew up all over the United States and in other countries as well. Their educational credentials range from trade school certificates to Ph.D.s, and they hold jobs as various as actress, corporate marketing manager, yoga teacher, graphic designer, high school counselor, environmental scientist, and hairdresser. Some of them knew from childhood that they were not interested in motherhood, while others fully expected to raise a family someday.

As different as they are, several similar threads run through their stories. These women speak of being drawn to many of life's wonderful paths and pleasures—art, activism, adventure, an intimate relationship with a husband or partner, scholarship, friendships, career, solitude, travel, spirituality. They are all leading fulfilling, productive lives. They're contributing and happy. They understand that they are different from the majority of women; their senses of identity, femininity, productivity, and security are not tied to motherhood, and they are comfortable with that difference.

Although the subtitle of this book refers to women without children, children figure prominently in several of the narrators' professional and personal lives. These women, however, aren't compensating for not bearing children of their own; rather, they often feel they have the best of both worlds. As the African proverb says,

"It takes a village to raise a child," and as members of the village—as aunts, teachers, doctors, ministers, therapists, and friends—many voluntarily childless women help raise and sometimes repair or rescue the next generation while retaining the personal freedom they find integral to their identities. This larger scope of nurturing, so fully satisfying to many childfree women, is often overlooked as the major contribution to society that it is.

The women in this book who are not involved with children live out the nurturing sides of themselves with other adults, animals, and nature, and many of them make a difference on global, national, and local fronts through their careers and volunteer work. Others have assumed pivotal roles in their families of origin in caring for family members who are ill or negotiating difficult life passages. Through their service to organizations and their families, these women increase their own sense of belonging and their connections to community and tribe. In reading the stories in this book, you'll see how stereotypical comments about childfree women—"You just hate kids" or "You're just selfish"—are unfounded.

During our meetings I was honored by the openness and honesty of all interviewees, how freely they talked about their family histories, intimate relationships, self-images, creative outlets, fears, ambitions, dreams, and authentic connections with children. Only two women requested anonymity out of concern for their family or professional situation, and I respected those requests; the rest were happy to tell their stories publicly, and some considered their chapter as a legacy they could pass on to others. About half of the women I interviewed had terminated a pregnancy, and although I decided not to include this information in their individual chapters, I must point out that their stories underscore how essential legal abortion is to a woman's choice not only about when, but also about whether, to bear children.

One of the biggest challenges in producing this book was conveying the "voices" of the women whose stories appear. I benefited from meeting and talking with each woman, hearing the inflection and tone of her voice, noting her chuckles and pauses, observing her facial expressions and gestures. I want you to feel a similar intimacy with these narrators, and I hope that my careful editing and their thorough reviews of their chapters help you to "hear" and "see" their levity and seriousness, their heartfelt comments as well as their lighthearted ones, their sarcasm and sparkle. I encourage you to draw your own conclusions about each of their stories and to draw inspiration and support from them as well.

While I didn't set out in search of it, I found joy and camaraderie in interviewing these childfree figures. Meeting 25 fascinating women who spoke with vivid voices about their happy lives packed a big wallop, and for three years I was on the receiving end of a steady flow of their engrossing stories. I left each interview energized. What a huge pool of female talent and energy and experience is out there, I often thought, and how interesting and important are its applications. What purpose, what contentment! What would it mean for our society, I wondered, if women without children were as valued and celebrated as mothers are?

THE WOMEN

Monica Harrington, 37, grew up in Portland, Oregon.
Her father was an attorney and her mother a homemaker.
She is the youngest of eight children.

Monica earned a bachelor's degree in journalism and
worked as an editor and in public relations before becoming a senior
marketing manager at a major software corporation.
She lives with Mike, her husband of seven years, plus two cats,
Max and The Foof Cat, and a springer spaniel puppy, Emma,
in a lodge-like country home overlooking a valley.

Monica enjoys the outdoors through horseback riding, hiking,
snowboarding, skiing, and boating and likes socializing with friends
and family. She also loves to read true-crime stories and historical
nonfiction and calls herself a "magazine junkie."

MONICA HARRINGTON

I walk, making up phrases; sit, contriving scenes; am, in short,

in the thick of the greatest rapture known to me.

VIRGINIA WOOLF

WHEN I WAS GROWING UP, MY IMAGE FOR my life resembled the roles that Katharine Hepburn played — women of high independence who lived life for themselves, not through other people. I had an aunt who didn't marry until she was over fifty, and she seemed to live an interesting life as a working woman in San Francisco. I suppose I thought of her as glamorous because she fit that Hepburn model, and I thought she was terrific.

As a girl I announced to my family that I was going to be "fixed" like a cat, so they all liked to joke about "Monica's attitude towards having children." And indeed I never gravitated toward babies or images of them. One year my mother tried to make up for not having many dolls around by giving me one for Christmas, complete with lots of clothes and accessories. I remember opening the packages and growing depressed, thinking, "Who are these for? Not me." In junior high the only option most girls had for making money was baby-sitting, and I wasn't the least interested, feeling quite glad when I was finally old enough to make money in other ways.

I came at the tail end of eight kids born one right after another, and I was eighteen when my older siblings started having children. I was around those kids a lot and could see that even under the best of circumstances, even for very nurturing types, motherhood is a real commitment and hard work, though it can bring tremendous rewards. One time a boyfriend and I took care of my brother's three young children for several days. These were terrific kids, I knew them well, and it was incredibly stressful. I wasn't used to the constant vigilance required, making sure that they were bathed, clothed, fed, and entertained. Caring for them really tired me out, but I knew I had to bump my energy to a higher level. And that's my image of parenthood: you've got to always be there and be up for your kids.

I dated casually until I was twenty-one because I was focused on school, but after that I started dating someone who clearly wanted children eventually. That wasn't a key part of our early conversations, but his offhand comments about a future family life made me uneasy, and I remember thinking, "That doesn't sound good to me." Yet it took a long time for me to regard this as a fundamental difference between us; the relationship went on for five years before I connected the dots and saw that we shouldn't be together.

I always assumed I would get married, and it never occurred to me that finding somebody who felt as I did about not having children might be difficult. I considered my view of the world—including the idea that life could hold more if I didn't have kids—as natural, but I realized that it is a minority view. The number of women and men who see things my way is smaller than I thought. After my boyfriend and I broke up, I made a career move to a new city and decided to no longer invest time in a relationship with a man unless we agreed about not having children. I think that decision had a huge amount to do with whom I met next—the man I would marry—and how our relationship proceeded.

Mike and I worked for the same company but we initially met and got to know each other by playing on a volleyball team. When we first started dating I thought the relationship would be short-term; he is four years younger than I, and to me, younger meant not ready for commitment—and that was fine with me at the time. Still, on some of our first dates we "interviewed" each other with questions like: What type of people have you dated? What do you want out of life? What about children? On this last point he told me that he had assumed he would be a father but wasn't bent on having kids. He felt flexible and interested in exploring what it would mean for his life not to become a father.

Along the way Mike and I had other conversations about kids, and at some point when we were getting serious I made it clear to him that I wasn't intending to have any. "I'm a package deal," I said. "If we decide to get married, then you're choosing not only me but a lifestyle, too. If you want children, then I'm not the right person for you." Obviously he chose me, and we're happy with our life together.

Mike is the center of my emotional life, and we're definitely cheerleaders for each other's careers. We genuinely like and love each other, and we talk four or five times a day from our offices, maybe just a two-minute call to share good news about work or to vent after a difficult meeting. We're always the one the other wants to turn to when something interesting happens.

Because we both have demanding jobs, we've established boundaries around work—like spending every weekend together and reserving Thursday as "date night." On summer weekends we go boating, on winter weekends we snowboard, and we take drives in the country and go for short getaways all year round.

Recently I spent a day or two with one of my brothers and his wife, who have a baby. I like kids, particularly my nieces and nephews, and I had a good time on this visit. A friend who was with us that weekend said to my sister-in-law, "Monica must want children. It's obvious she likes them." I thought that was an interesting comment, because for me what's obvious is the separation of ideas: I like kids, but more as little people than as people I want to take care of.

Even though I haven't wavered from my image for a life without motherhood, I've never considered sterilization because I like the idea that I'm constantly making choices about how I want to live. Nothing I foresee would make parenting an attractive choice for me, and I would be astounded if I ever did an about-face on that, yet I leave this remote possibility intact. My oldest sister didn't have kids until she was in her thirties, and a few friends who shared similar views to mine about parenting changed their minds and had kids. Those events showed me that it's important to keep my options open, that the life I want today may not necessarily be the life I'll want tomorrow. I will also say that I'm probably the most careful person on the planet about contraception: I grew up in a time where people had sex at a pretty early age, and I can tell you that I have never had unprotected sex, never in my life.

Because having children is the majority experience, we women who don't want to have kids sometimes experience pressure to change our minds. Some people think a woman's life can't be fulfilled unless she has kids, and they have a negative attitude about childlessness. Among my friends who have had children, several seem to want me to join their "club" as they begin to relate more with the woman down the street who has a child than they do with me. Some get quite evangelical!

I tell close friends that I'm not planning on having children but I'm not a crusader for the childfree life. That said, I also think that a lot more people should seriously consider not having children. It's pretty clear from everything we see around us that people who probably shouldn't be having children are. Some people are temperamentally not suited to parenthood, but because childlessness isn't encouraged as a viable choice, they don't get to explore it. Others go on automatic pilot and have children, and sometimes they're not happy with the kids they get or the family lifestyle.

When I see situations like that I think, "What a waste! What if they'd been able to think things through consciously and make a choice that was a better fit for who they really are?" Society would be better served if some people who were truly cut out and prepared for parenthood and really wanted kids had four or five of them and those who weren't didn't have any.

My generation of women is the first to enjoy the real possibility of a meaningful career. In the past, women didn't have these opportunities; generally, if a woman was married and fertile, she had children and stayed home with them. A few women had careers, but they were pioneers. Today professional women are not a phenomenon, they're mainstream.

My work stimulates me. I regularly have exhilarating, fun conversations with senior public relations executives from the top agencies in the country in which we discuss media and marketing trends and what's exciting about my company's products. For me, work combines many areas of personal interest—reading magazines and books and keeping on top of current trends like the hot TV shows, issues people are concerned about, and what's going on in politics. In my job, understanding the public pulse is an asset, so all the reading I do in my leisure time helps me to be more effective in my work.

Because my professional life is important to me, I appreciate that not having kids gives me more flexibility at work; I don't have to consider childcare when it comes to traveling or what hours I'm at the office. Mike works odd hours too, often late into the night, and we negotiate our schedules depending upon what we have planned, what friends we're seeing, when we want to be together. We like this arrangement, and it would be impossible if we were raising children.

When I read about an author who writes a book that breaks through the hordes of published titles, I wonder what the writing life would be like—very solitary and very rewarding, I imagine. In a desk drawer at home I keep notes about stories and articles I want to write, and at some point, I expect I will say to myself, "OK, I've really enjoyed marketing; now it's time to do this other thing because I don't want to look back and wish I would have done it." For some people this "other thing" might be having children, but for me it's writing. If I never write, I know I'll regret it.

At some point I may work for myself in order to have more free time to connect with people and animals. I may not have a strong maternal instinct when it comes to children but I'm very bonded to our animals. Recently I was at a book club meeting where one of the women, who has children, commented that she's relieved she doesn't have pets. As an animal lover I was stung, and my reaction was, "But you miss so much!" Then it occurred to me, "She's passionate about her kids, I'm passionate about my animals. Neither of us would choose to trade places with the other, and that's the way it should be."

In the future when I'm working less, I'll also spend time volunteering for organizations that I consider important and now support financially. Working for money isn't the guiding principle of my life; working at something I'm passionate about is. I believe that success follows doing something you love. I've had financial success, and if in the future I do work that isn't financially successful, I expect it to be soul-satisfying.

I imagine that when Mike and I are middle-aged, we will still be a passionate couple with independent and shared interests. We may be activists, traveling, experiencing life, talking and arguing. The funny part is that when I fast-forward to old age, I see myself alone. . . . When I'm old I'll have some cool friends whom I'll enjoy getting together with, and I'll still be actively involved in the world around me, still engaged. I see myself in a house in a beautiful setting, writing, having travel adventures interspersed with home time. That's my idea of a good life.

Maggie Lindley, 48, was born in London. Her father was a doctor
and her mother a registered nurse. She has a younger brother.

Maggie left England at age 18 to travel around Europe and Africa.
After that she worked in North America in the maritime industry for
about 20 years, fishing commercially; building, repairing,
and sailing boats; and underwriting policies for a corporate marine
insurance carrier. Three years ago Maggie cruised to the South Pacific
with friends on a 50-foot catamaran that she helped to build.

Following a vision of combining her love of boats with another
passion—food—Maggie is now in culinary school, hoping eventually to
work as a chef on recreational charter boats. She lives with
two roommates and enjoys hiking, sailing, fine dining, and cooking.

MAGGIE LINDLEY

I cannot count the good people I know who to my mind would be even better if they bent their spirits to the study of their own hungers.

M.F.K. FISHER

THERE WERE PROBABLY MORE ROLE MODELS for childlessness in England when I was growing up than in the States, maybe because so many Englishmen died in World War II. The postwar years were very poor, very depressing, and children were an economic burden. I remember hearing about how expensive it was to raise a family, and couples without children weren't uncommon.

During my teenage years I read magazines galore, and the images that appealed to me then featured beautiful people enjoying themselves on big yachts floating in blue water under sunny skies. I knew I wanted to have adventures like that and be happy. And while my life hasn't exactly followed that picture, it has a lot in common with it!

Probably also because of the things I was reading at the time, I remember saying that I wanted to meet a starving artist and live with him in a garret. The American man I met in my late teens was a sculptor who didn't have any money, and we did live in an interesting place in southern England that had hand-painted Victorian wallpaper—it was above an arcade that had pinball machines going constantly! So in various ways I have gotten what I saw for myself in my youth.

In the early seventies I was in Alaska, then traveled in Europe and Africa, and in my mid-twenties I went to Canada to be with friends who were building a boat and running a group home for troubled kids. My friends' place was home to four or five kids ranging in age from eight to fifteen. The kids went to school during the day, and my friends and I worked on the boat during those hours. I also relieved my friends, living at the house for forty-eight hours at a time while they took a break.

In essence, during those weekends I became a single parent to several kids with bad attitudes. I was tough enough to take it but also open enough to see—and it was apparent from every story they told—that these children had been unwanted and ultimately rejected by their parents. Many were from split homes, and from what I could tell, most of them would be perpetuating the cycle. Our job was to try to break the cycle, but the kids were pretty set on doing to others exactly what had been done to them. I was not encouraged by all I saw there to have children myself.

In my mid-thirties I spent seven years in relationship with a man who had been very clear with me that he did not want children, and that had felt perfectly OK with me. When I was forty-three, my doctor told me I needed a hysterectomy. I was scared at the thought of anesthesia, scalpels, and a hospital stay, and I was confronted with my own mortality and the sweetness of life. Both to rest and to exercise my mind before surgery, I went on a ten-day personal-growth workshop aboard a Caribbean cruise ship. Because the hysterectomy was imminent, I was thinking about not having kids and the rightness to me of that choice. I talked to one instructor about it, and she said, "Oh, you'll have plenty of children." I took that to mean that I would have plenty of people to nurture.

The surgery went fine and was a defining moment physically because the decision not to have children was at that point absolute. It would have been interesting to experience being pregnant and giving birth because natural processes fascinate me. I remember a young Brazilian friend who was very beautiful and very comfortable with her body. She had caramel-colored skin, and during her pregnancy she showed me how her belly expanded down this whitish line from her navel to her pubic hair. What a physically amazing transformation! I am equally amazed by caterpillars in cocoons that later turn into butterflies.

That said, I don't regret my choice not to have a child. As I grow older I'm realizing that I have to acknowledge and release a number of experiences that I haven't had and won't have; that's part of aging gracefully. When I think back on my traveling days in Africa, for instance—sleeping outside for six weeks, and all those tanned, strong male bodies I got to meet and hang out with—I have to release the idea that I could go and do it all over again. I was there, but I've moved on. I celebrate that I had the experience and don't resent the fact that it won't come again. I shall never travel in that same style, and I'm aware that to be with a young man today is possible but no longer appropriate. It wouldn't teach me what I need to learn now.

I'm aware that some women with children envy the life that I have, and I see the life that they have and think theirs is wonderful, too. But it doesn't look so wonderful that I wish I had gone that way. I've avoided the white picket fence, and sometimes I ask myself, "Is it alright that I lived this other way?" When I look at all the brush strokes that make up the painting of my life, when I allow myself to feel the passion that's moved me on to various courses, I see the answer is "Yes." I see that my choices were inspired by something within me, such as the overwhelming desire to live "off the grid" by traveling and going to sea. There were days that I woke up and knew I had to go on a long boat ride and see horizon all around me. I can tell you it was far more compelling than waking up and saying, "I need to go to the mall today"!

My history is intertwined with the times in which I've lived—so much so that I'm not sure how much I have influenced my life's events or how much the events have influenced me. A good example: When I was a teenager there were no incurable sexually transmitted diseases, birth control became readily available, and I took full advantage of both those circumstances. In the last how many thousands of years, how many women have been in that fortunate situation?

In the late seventies I lived in San Francisco, and the consciousness there at that time was very spiritual. Self-knowledge, personal growth, spirituality, the search for the meaning of life—these things that have always been very important to me—were front and center in California, too, and I participated in various workshops and study groups there. Some friends with whom I've spent a lot of time have a nine-year-old son, and when I've visited them at home I've seen that in a family setting, life is life and the next meal is the next meal and the next batch of laundry is the next batch of laundry. Having kids doesn't leave a lot of time to ponder the meaning of life, and, for me, having time to ponder life's questions has always been essential.

Not having children gives me a lot of options that women with children don't have, including options related to having economic control of my life. Since I'm the only person I have to support, my decisions regarding work are based only on my needs, which aren't that great. I can choose to work part-time or to live off savings for a while if I want to take time away from work altogether. Children require a different focus—more stability, a home, schools, health insurance, a whole different setup than I need to have—and so their parents have to do what it takes to maintain that focus.

I have a friend whom I didn't hear from much for five years while she was raising two little boys. Eventually she called and said, "I'm beginning to emerge from googoogaagaaland." This woman was educated and very developed spiritually and personally, yet for five years she was focused entirely on providing the basics for two little humans. When we were able to spend time together again, she seemed to see me as a welcome visitor from the adult world, and it was my opportunity to learn something about the world she was inhabiting.

I don't think that my mother, who died eighteen years ago, ever entered googoogaagaaland, and I believe if she had it to do over, she wouldn't have kids. That's just a feeling because she never said anything to that effect, but she had an analytical mind and lived a rich intellectual life. I think she had children because she saw it as a function society expected her to perform. But she never told me that she thought I should do the same.

My father, however, thought that was exactly what I should do. The British aren't very good at saying things directly, but when I moved out of the house at eighteen to live with Paul, my American boyfriend, I could tell that my father was devastated. My mother told me how upset he was that I was living with a man I wasn't married to; at the time, that just wasn't done. My father didn't cut me out of his life, but he never visited Paul and me. I realized then that he had very different plans for me—plans that included a conventional life of marriage and children. In my mid-twenties I came back to England from Alaska to visit. I had money and fishing tales, and my father started to think of me in a *National Geographic* sense, as more of a person of the world than as a live-around-the-corner type. But it wasn't until much later that I learned to connect with him without old feelings of teenage rebellion, and that he and I met as adults.

My brother is married with two children and lives near Dad, and perhaps his traditional life helped my father accept my unconventional one. Today my dad and I get along famously, and he sees I'm happy with the choices I've made.

Creating bonds of friendship is important to me, and I sustain them over distance and time. When we've been apart, my friends are as thrilled to see me as I am to reconnect with them. I suppose that for me these deep friendships take the place of that specifically directed passion that a mother has for a child. I attend to and nurture my friends. I call. I write. I say, "Hi, I'm here. This is what's happening with me. What's going on with you? Are you healthy? Are you happy? Do things look good for the future?" I believe a nurturing instinct can be focused on one or two individuals, as mothers do with their children, or spread out more widely than that.

Reading is another passion of mine. Books were an incredible consolation to me when I was a teenager—learning that I wasn't the only one who felt the way I felt about various things was such a relief. Someday I'd like to write from my own life—stories that detail what I've learned, the ups and downs, the surprising places I've found inspirational. I might like to dramatize real events from my life, such as the commercial fishing adventures, the sailing cruise to Samoa, different situations that I ended up in simply by going for it—going for the money, going for the romance, going for the novelty, going for the sex, going away from where I was to someplace else.

Food is a whole fascinating and creative area I've just begun to tap into. My mother had a passion for French food—the haute cuisine of England at the time I was growing up there—and she was always preparing tournedos Rossini and other exotic dishes for the family. And when I worked in the financial district in San Francisco, one of my motivations for climbing the corporate ladder was that it was the only way I could take clients to all the wonderful restaurants downtown!

Now I'm in cooking school and I love it. Going to school has been a great achievement for me, and it's shown me how many ways there are to expend my energy, how many options there always are for the next step in my growth. In some ways my head is as full of potential adventures as it was when I was eighteen, and I think that's because I still have the option to move toward and fulfill dreams if they are compelling enough. It seems that men have always had that freedom, whereas women's dreams often collapse under the weight of obligation to their children.

Over the next few years I expect to put some things—housing, money, and so on—in place to sustain me later in my life. My dream job is to go to Alaska as a chef on an exclusive charter boat, and I imagine that for the next ten years or so I'll be cooking—if not on the water, then perhaps on land, in a restaurant or retirement home.

For the rest of my working years, I want jobs that allow me to be content but not bored and that give me time to think and write.

When I'm old I'll want to be around people, ideally some sort of extended family or community that includes small children, middle-aged adults, teenagers, other old people. In planning for their old age, some friends of mine have built a co-housing community, and that concept is quite appealing to me.

I was making a collage recently from images cut from cooking and sailing magazines. By chance one of the images I found was a picture of a classic eighty-foot sailing yacht from the 1930s. These sailors are wearing baggy pants, looking sort of like the America's Cup of the old days, and they are heeled over, obviously going to weather.

In this photo is a woman who's in her sixties or older; she's on the leeward side of the boat, just staring straight ahead. She's a sailor, out with all these young men, and the photo suggests it's important to them that she's there and important to her to be there as well. I thought, "What a cool image!" It helped me believe that I can sail in the future—that is, even when the body slows down, I will still have my knowledge and experience to offer. I can still be part of things.

Angie Bolton, 43, grew up in Athens, Georgia.
Her mother was a nurse, and her dad was a carpenter and
later a jewelry engraver. She is an only child.

Angie was in the third class of women who went to Yale,
and she has a bachelor's degree in drama. For 17 years she has acted,
sung, and danced as a member of Tickle Tune Typhoon,
"a rock-and-roll band for children and family entertainment,"
which performs all over the United States and has produced seven
recordings and a video. Angie has been an artist-in-residence,
teaching creative movement in elementary, junior high,
and high schools, and she also appears in local adult productions.
To supplement her income, she teaches aerobics classes for senior citizens.

Angie has lived with her husband, Dan, for 16 years.
She loves to read science fiction, mysteries, magazines, and
newspapers and to watch movies and TV.

ANGIE BOLTON

The work of art which I do not make, none other will ever make.

SIMONE WEIL

PROBABLY BECAUSE I'M AN ONLY CHILD, AS a girl whenever I imagined myself as a grownup I pictured myself alone. Some only children crave having kids but I never did. My mother is also an only child, and my dad had two sisters with no children, so at family gatherings I was the only young one. Because I was used to having conversations with adults, I didn't relate to people of my own age very well. Only as an adult, when I began performing for kids and got to know some of my friends' children, did I come to appreciate kids and enjoy their company.

As I was growing up I could see how the church and my family wanted to influence my direction. My mother is a spiritual person and frustrated, I think, by an unfulfilled need to be a preacher. I went to church with her until I was about fifteen, then I said,

"That's it." Accepting the dogma became too difficult for me—no church was going to tell me to have babies just because some book of scriptures says to "be fruitful and multiply."

I can remember that around the same time my mother mentioned that she was looking forward to being a grandma. I pointed out to her that she was putting pressure on me to be a certain way for her benefit, and I said, "Maybe you ought to have had more kids and not put all your eggs in one basket. . . ." Maybe I knew at fifteen that I wouldn't have kids and wanted to prepare her for that. My grandmother, who lived with us when I was young, also had dreams for me that may have included children; she wanted me to go farther than she had yet also wanted me to further the race and make things better for people of our ethnic and cultural background.

Someone once said to me that they thought it selfish of me, an educated African-American woman, not to have children. They were adamant that I should carry on the race, that I wasn't being responsible in my choices regarding work, populating, and educating people of color. I think that comment springs from the general idea that each of us should give back to the community in some way, and we can all agree with that. But often it's assumed that women will give back by having children and making them into community leaders. For me it's hard to be seen as selfish for not having children, to be regarded as being all for myself rather than as doing other things in the community that need to be done.

The weight of all that socialization and expectation! At times I feel angry about it, and sometimes I feel guilty about letting people down. But I can only be who I am, and if people don't like it, then they don't like it.

In college I read quite a bit of women's literature and started viewing our social structures differently. I started seeing how women were saddled with children, often primarily responsible for raising them, and usually forced by the need for two incomes to hold down a job outside the home as well. Yet even though women may work outside the home, they still do the lion's share of work inside the home. I decided I was not going to live like that.

Throughout my late twenties and thirties I kept pushing motherhood away, thinking, "Not now, not now!" I suppose I thought there would come a time later when I would want to have kids, but later never came. Today when I see infants, I sometimes think, "Ooh, that's a nice, bright smile," but I also think, "Ooh, get up at all hours of the night, feed them, gotta earn enough money to pay for schools and clothes." I recognize how much having kids impacts your life, and the drive was never strong enough to win out. Luckily this hasn't been an issue for Dan. He and I got together in our mid-twenties, and we've had only a few conversations about whether we'd have kids or not. The way it comes up is that we'll see a mixed-race kid and ask each other, "Wow, would our kids look like that?"

Dan directs a nonprofit organization that serves artists with disabilities, and he's also a musician, currently playing in a band. Since we're both involved in performing, we can both get overwhelmed by exhaustion, and that can sometimes make our life as a couple and our bond difficult to sustain.

For example, we don't make the time to socialize with our friends as often as we should. But we share at least one meal a day, we go to neighborhood restaurants, and we like to see movies or watch videos. Friends with children tell me that the exhaustion of parenting is unbelievable and makes life as a couple almost impossible to put first. By the time you feed the kids and get them in bed, all you're going to talk about is who's taking the kids to school and who's picking them up from daycare. Everything else gets tabled until it blows up and you're yelling at each other.

Dan and I are so outwardly engaged with our work that sometimes we just come home and sit quietly together to recharge our batteries or read the newspaper or watch TV. My life is so full, I'm grateful I don't have someone who's dependent on me, who I always have to crank it up for. When I come home from work, there's no toddler who needs to be fed, washed, picked up after. I put out for people all day long, and it's hard to imagine having to do it all night long and every weekend too.

If Dan had said at some point that he wanted children, I would have had to discuss it with him, given that we've been together for so long. I certainly would not have said, "Forget it, goodbye," because we're very, very good friends. Sometimes couples stay together for the sake of their children, but couples who don't have children have to be very good friends if they're going to endure.

A few years ago I thought I saw signs that Dan was wanting kids, so I asked him, "What's going on?" When we got to the nitty-gritty questions about how our lives would have to change if we had a child—Which of us would give up our creative work to take care of the kid? Who would go out and make some serious money?—the idea didn't look so wonderful to him. In our marriage I'm the practical one, and on big questions I find myself saying to Dan, "Let's look a little closer at this."

Last year I was faced with the possibility of a hysterectomy because of fibroid tumors. As illogical as it may sound, it was a difficult moment because, for me, it's different to choose not to have children than to have childlessness dictated by my physical circumstance. I found myself feeling betrayed by my body, which had always had the capacity for childbearing, even if I had not chosen to use it. Ultimately that experience gave me more compassion for women who want to conceive and whose bodies don't cooperate.

Picasso said, "It takes a very, very long time to become young," and it took years of being around kids for me to understand what kids are about. I didn't set out to perform for children but I've come to appreciate my career. Over seventeen years, through artist-in-residencies in schools and performing with Tickle Tune Typhoon, I've touched a lot of kids' lives. And I love the response I get from them. They react to me the same way adults react to Mick Jagger! Performing for kids has helped me reconnect with the youthful part of myself that used to dance around the room, make faces in the mirror, sing along with the radio. It's helped me feel more carefree about my life and taught me how to play.

From working in schools, I see that some parents today are creating a lot of needy children, and those children will go on to create more needy children. Many parents are so stressed out by their own lives, so uneducated about how to rear children, so afraid of setting boundaries that they're raising feral, violent youths who travel in packs. It's frightening. I have a sense of social responsibility, and I'd like to help out in this crisis. Short of taking a child into my home, I see ways that I can assist: I might become a Big Sister or volunteer to tutor a child at my neighborhood elementary school. When I interact with certain kids, I may be more effective than their parents because the kids can't push my buttons.

I've worked hard to make a living as a professional performer, and for several years I haven't been the generative artist I was in my twenties, when I wrote my own material and did improvisational pieces. As I've aged I've become fearful of falling on my face, and I'm trying to get back into my young, courageous mode.

Toward that end I'm now in two shows with a local adult company, and I'm adapting one of my short stories into a play.

If I had a kid I'd be thinking about putting him through college, not about the next step in my career. But because I'm free to develop my talents, I'm taking an acting class to push myself toward TV and film. Roles for middle-aged and older women of color are few and far between, and I've realized that if I want to perform such roles I'll have to write them. I want to interview people in my senior aerobics classes; even from the little bit I know about them, I can tell their stories are rich and could be mined for characters that I could create for the screen.

I imagine that even when I become a cantankerous old lady, I'll do volunteer outreach work, and maybe it will include performing. I'll live in a little house, doing my thing, gardening, trying to help children or other seniors somehow. One way to get really old before your time is to just stop—to stay at home and fail to stimulate your mind—so I'll continue to teach exercise classes for as long as I can. I'll read, spend time with kids, do yoga. I'll be satisfied.

Jane Smiley, 72, grew up in New Jersey.
Her mother was an amateur pianist and her father sold advertising for
several national magazines. She has a younger brother.

Like the prize-winning author of the same name,
Jane has had a distinguished career. She spent about 20 years in retail
at large department stores, beginning as an assistant buyer and,
at the end of her career, as vice president of special events and public
relations for a major chain. In the middle of her career she was on staff
for 21 years at The New Yorker, first in ad sales and later as the
magazine's fashion and retail advertising consultant. She has
a bachelor's degree in government and art history from Smith College.

Jane enjoys volunteering with local arts organizations,
a women's center, and a college foundation. A widow, she lives
in a high-rise waterfront condo filled with original art she has collected.
She travels extensively and socializes with friends and family.

JANE T. SMILEY

When a woman falls in love with the magnificent

possibilities within herself, the forces that would limit those

possibilities hold less and less sway over her.

MARIANNE WILLIAMSON

IN MY FAMILY, CHILDREN WEREN'T PATTED on the head and told how beautiful they were. We were raised to think about what we were doing, our roles in the community. My father was on the school board, my mother was active, and during the war we rolled bandages for the Red Cross and cultivated our victory gardens. My mother was a cool cat, unemotional. My father was similar and very practical. He sent me to shop school with my brother and taught us both how to use guns. I learned how to put storm windows on the house and chains on the car, how to sail and to ride horses. After I was grown, my parents never said beans to me about the choices I made for my life—except for becoming a Democrat, which they

29

didn't care for. If they ever had any opinion about my not having children, they kept it to themselves.

Although my parents never coached me in this direction, in general the women of my generation were raised to believe they were going to get married and have kids. But somehow I knew that even if I did marry and become a mother, I would work. By the time I was in college I knew that I was smart and that I didn't want to be a teacher or nurse or any of the hand-holding professions because I'm not a nurturer. I like to run things! I have always been interested in design, color, and fashion, so I decided to go into merchandising. In 1947, after the war, all the New York department stores were interviewing, and I got into an executive training program at the most desired spot: Macy's.

A few years into that program, though, I started having second thoughts about being in retail and thought perhaps I should be doing the things my college friends were doing—getting married and accepting invitations to join the Junior League. So I quit my job and moved back to the suburbs. When I left Macy's, my manager said, "You're doing the right thing. I'm twenty-nine, I don't have a boyfriend, and I'm working twenty-four hours a day. This is a tough job. Go home and get married."

After I moved I got an interesting position in advertising research, but soon I'd had enough of the suburbs. I'd go to cocktail parties, and I couldn't talk business with the men because they wouldn't let a woman join in a business conversation, and I couldn't talk babies with the women. I felt like the odd person out. It didn't take long to know that I never wanted to live in the suburbs again, and I went back to New York City.

In my late twenties I had lots of beaux, and I could have married any of them. But something slowed me down, and I wasn't falling madly in love with any of the guys I dated. They were nice, we would go out and have a good time, and that was that. And I didn't feel maternal; nothing was pushing me, no inner voice was saying, "Don't you want to have kids?"

When I worked for *The New Yorker,* my job involved traveling throughout the United States, surveying for quality merchandise and talking with newspaper and marketing and advertising people, chambers of commerce, and merchants. I physically shopped the better stores in all of the markets where *The New Yorker* magazine reader would be apt to shop. I traveled first class, and all the entertaining we did was absolutely deluxe because it was in the style of *The New Yorker* magazine. I met wonderful people and had a great time. It was marvelous.

In my New York business world, we women were all active professionally and socially. Many of us didn't have children, and those who did didn't talk about them. I recall one woman colleague who had children and did the train commute to and from the suburbs with the men. She was a sharp dresser and a lovely person, but her after-work life didn't look interesting to me.

Part of my job when I was in New York City was to invite visiting VIPs to my apartment for cocktails, then take them to dinner. One time in 1964 I was planning such a party and invited a few of my girlfriends as well as the out-of-town guests. One friend asked if she could bring a date—her ex-husband, as it turned out, in whom she was still interested—and I said, "Fine, bring him along."

We all went out to dinner and to someone's place afterwards to dance. This friend's ex-husband and I danced together, and I found him very attractive. The following Friday evening she brought him to another small black-tie party, and later at a club he and I danced the twist. He asked me out, and it was the last date I ever went on. We married four months later.

I was thirty-nine when we married, and the first thing my boss said to me after the wedding was, "As soon as you get pregnant, go to England and get a nanny. Don't talk to the child until it's twenty years old." I don't remember precisely how I responded to that, except to say I doubted I would be having children.

Dick had five marvelous children by his first two wives. At the time we married, his children were ages twenty-one, nineteen, sixteen, four, and two. The second wife—my by-now-estranged friend—and the younger kids moved out of town after Dick and I married, and we didn't see much of them, which was a shame. Later, when those kids grew up, they were receptive to a relationship with me. The older children lived with their mom and came into the city on weekends to visit. I grew very fond of all the children and am still close to them. Today they live around the country, and we visit each other at holidays and other times. The older ones are parents themselves, so I have "grandchildren."

Dick and I had an upside-down marriage. He was a brilliant man, a voracious reader with a great intellect, but he didn't have a career. Instead he took on temporary jobs to help his kids out with college expenses, and he took care of our household. We had a nice social life, put on productions with a comedy club Dick belonged to, and went to Europe every year.

By the mid-seventies I had been with *The New Yorker* for two decades and felt it was time for a change. I was offered a good job in retail that involved relocating to Florida. The move was full of nervousness because Dick and I were New Yorkers through and through and wondered how life elsewhere would be, but it worked out fine. I retired in 1991 at age sixty-six just as Dick, who had had cancer for seven years, was told that he had a year to live.

We went off to have our last fling in Europe, but after four weeks in France, things grew too difficult for him and we came home.

Dick's health went downhill the following spring, and all the children came to see him. It was so hard to watch this big man failing. He passed away eleven months after I retired, and we had a ceremony in a friend's backyard. All his kids came again, and I spread his ashes in the friend's rose garden.

Unfortunately I don't go out with men at this point in my life, but I really would like to have a male friend who lived in my building. Some of my friends have loves who do not live with them but live instead in their own apartments. For all intents and purposes they are a couple; they see each other all the time and travel together. I'd like to fall in love again.

I think about growing old alone. Dick's eldest daughter talks about moving here, and I'd love to have her near. But as close as I am to all these children I've mentioned, I don't know that they want responsibility for me. My brother and his wife have talked about buying an apartment in my building, and the three of us being together would be helpful. The idea of falling down in my apartment when I'm alone is not a happy thought, and I'm only seventy-two.

I have a feeling that down the road I'll end up in the kind of place where you have a room or apartment of your own, there's a community dining room, and you're taken care of. My mother, who lived to be ninety-nine, resided in such a place, then spent her last three months in a nursing home. I have enough money to live on in my older years, and it should buy decent options. I have a luxury car now, which I never allowed myself before, and I still have a beautiful wardrobe. But I live within my means.

For today I like to keep busy, going to educational lectures on international subjects, current events, and the arts. I also love to travel. My last trip was to Poland, Prague, and East Germany. I've been to Russia twice, first in 1961 and then in 1992—what a contrast! The second time, I was invited by a Russian women's union to talk to women writers and artists and discuss health care. It was fascinating!

While I was in business, I liked to mentor other women. I helped several girls climb the ladder and have been their friend. We were all career-driven, and although one or two of them were mothers, children weren't a part of our discussions, not even as an aside. I don't think the mothers talked with each other much about their kids, and they never did with me. That was fine, because I was concentrating on developing their thinking about their careers. I'm still in contact with them, and we see each other from time to time. That's been very satisfying.

As a professional, I helped to arrange benefits for charities, but that's not the same as being a pure unpaid volunteer, as I am now. I'm on the boards of the local arts council and a women's center that offers career counseling to displaced homemakers. I'm past president of a college fund-raising organization, I volunteer hands-on for the food bank, and I'm the liaison from the arts council to the volunteer center. Ask me to join a committee where I can think, and I'll help.

What I'm doing now is based on my love of art and my community and my passion for helping women, and it's far more important than anything I did in the past. I have a full life, a very good life. I'm lucky, I'm happy, and I have no regrets.

Kris Romero, 48, grew up in a small city in Texas.
Her mother was a housewife and her father was a groundskeeper
at a military base. She is the eldest of five children.

Kris has a bachelor's degree in behavioral science
and a master's degree in social work. She has worked in evaluation of
the chronically mentally ill and also in human resources,
and she currently works for a city government as a personnel generalist.
She lives with Diane, her partner of five years, and their dogs Aja
and Monty and cats Keesha, Louise, and Luke.

By the time she learned to drive, Kris had developed a passion
for sports cars —she has owned an MG, a Triumph Spitfire,
and a Jaguar XKE—and would love to have been a race-car driver.
She is also a rock hound who loves fossils and crystals.

KRIS ROMERO

If we are to achieve a richer culture, rich in contrasting values,
we must recognize the whole gamut of human potentialities,
and so weave a less arbitrary social fabric,
one in which each diverse human gift will find a fitting place.

MARGARET MEAD

WHEN I WAS A TEENAGER I HATED SCHOOL. I believed that when I finished high school, that was going to be it. Then after graduation I worked in a factory—what a rude awakening! I quickly saw that I could not do menial work the rest of my life. A friend who'd gone away to junior college was writing to me, encouraging me to join her there, and even though I didn't know what I wanted to study, I thought, "I'll go."

Taking survey courses led me to the behavioral sciences, and there I found my passion. I was good at working with people, and I wanted to help in some way; I decided to become a psychiatric social worker. During college I worked for a private, nonprofit organization serving developmentally disabled adults, and I loved working there so much that I knew I was on the right track. I was the first in my family to graduate from college.

Today I'm happy with what I've accomplished professionally in assisting people. Here's an example: When I was working with developmentally disabled adults, I placed a man named Joseph in a pot-washing job at a local hospital. Being borderline retarded, that's about all he could do. The hospital had high turnover in the job, and I was able to persuade them that Joseph would probably hang in there with it, wouldn't get bored, wouldn't be quitting for a higher-paying job.

That happened in 1975, and Joseph still works there, soon to retire. He made a contribution to society that few others would: twenty-plus years of washing kettles in a hospital, never missing a day of work, never complaining. Joseph didn't talk much, was never in anyone's way. He just did his job, and his co-workers loved him. He earned his own way, got his own apartment, bought the best TV and sofa he could afford. I placed other clients like Joseph, and they made me very proud.

My specialty is the vocational side of social work. When the mental health center where I worked closed its cafeteria, I started a restaurant there offering job training for my clients. Many of my schizophrenic clients who never had been able to hold down a job—some who never had worked at all—had a good experience at Café del Sol. I had fun setting up the restaurant, it made money, and my clients learned that they could work and love it. They took great pride in the restaurant, and so did I.

Because my mom was sickly and my dad always worked two jobs to support so many kids, I almost single-handedly raised a few of my siblings, who were from three to ten years younger than I. I did the whole routine—fed them, bathed them, rocked them to sleep, walked them around the block in the stroller when they wouldn't go to sleep.

Once I became an adult I realized that I'd lost my own childhood in taking care of kids, and I didn't want any of my own. I knew the responsibility of motherhood and I'd had my fill of it. I also knew that if I had kids, I would probably raise them the way I was raised, not hesitating to give them a spanking if they were acting up, and I didn't want to repeat that.

But when I approached forty I wondered, "Am I going to be sorry about this decision?" Turning forty was a watershed in my life. That year I was thinking about how I hadn't achieved all I'd wanted in my career and wondering if I still could manage to do that. I was thinking about buying a home and about having only twenty years left to put into a career if I retire at sixty, as I'd like to.

As if all that wasn't enough, I revisited the issue of children as well. Luckily I asked myself the right question: Why would I have kids now? And the answers boiled down to selfishness: I wondered what a child of mine would look like, and I thought old age would be easier if there were a child around to care for me. I love kids, yet I wasn't contemplating having kids for the joy of having kids. No, it was all about narcissism and ego and fear.

Once I thought it through, it was easy to accept the decision I'd made earlier. The only piece still left is, When I get old, who'll care for me? That bothers me a bit, and so I jokingly lay the guilt trip on my nephews and nieces: "Aunt Kris has been really good to you!" When they were little I'd turn into a kid myself and act silly with them, playing, making up stories, taking them to Chuck E Cheese or to the park. When they were teens I acted like a teenager, goofing off with them. I'm very into cars and sports so I've always had that in common with my nephews, and we've done all kinds of things together related to those interests.

I feel I've left a mark with my siblings and their kids, helping them all become who they are. The nephew I'm closest to went into the personnel field and is now employed as a social worker with troubled kids at a Native American boys' home. Did he follow my lead there? I don't know. I do know he's sensitive and caring, with a heart of pure gold, and is perfectly suited to that work.

Before Diane and I moved in together, she talked about adopting a child and being a single mom. She seriously looked into it, and I was scared because I didn't feel like I could influence her or say anything to stop it. At the same time I knew that if Diane adopted a child, it would affect us negatively. It wouldn't have diminished my interest in her—I'm so in love, and I had wanted to be with her for so long—but it would have made our relationship rocky.

Diane didn't pursue adoption at that point, but about two years ago, after we moved in together, she proposed that we adopt a child together. Even though I had made my decision years before, a piece of me felt, "I want her to be happy, and if she wants children, that should be fine." But in the end I had to be truthful. I had to say to her, "If you want this, then do it, but you're on your own because I really don't want to. I don't have the energy to parent, so don't expect anything of me. If that's OK with you, then I guess it's OK with me."

Had Diane gone ahead with an adoption, frankly I don't think our relationship would have withstood it. Even though she might have thought she had enough energy for both of us, to say that is one thing but to live it is another. We don't even walk the dogs like we should! Take two careers, household chores, pets, now a career change for her that involves school on top of a job, then throw a kid into that mix, and something has to give: housework doesn't get done, animals aren't cared for, the guilt starts to mount, there's no "down time" together, and everybody's exhausted.

Diane and I decided not to add a child to our home, and every now and then I check in on how that decision is resting with her. I hope she doesn't blame me one day, doesn't feel sorry that she let me influence her, doesn't think, "I would have kids but for you." She wouldn't say such a thing, but the thought could still be in her heart—and I don't want any pain in her heart. I think the way she's resolved this is by meeting her need to nurture in many other ways. There are millions of children out there dying for the adult attention and affection that she can offer.

I fear getting old, and facing my fiftieth birthday is traumatic. I don't think I'll ever be old-thinking, but of course I'll slow down, wrinkle, lose my energy. I hope I'm in good enough spirits to accept what might go along with aging: illnesses, breaking a hip, a nursing home, all those difficult things. My great-grandmother, whom I adored, lived to be one hundred and one. I have the genes to live a long time, and I just hope it's quality time.

I'm looking forward to my retirement years. I've had so much responsibility in my life that I yearn to experience freedom. In a sense, retirement will be like getting to live my adolescence over again; I can sleep in, go to the park, hang out with friends as I please. By that age I'll have acquired the things I want—and I doubt I'll be able to get in and out of two-seater sports cars anymore, so that fetish will be resolved! Diane teases me about looking forward to retirement prematurely. She's ramping up with a new career, and although I've recently felt a new spark about my work as I move into management, I'm also gearing down some.

I love my nieces and nephews and their children so much that ultimately I'd like to end up near where some of them are living. And hopefully they'll be happy to have old Aunt Kris around.

Joan Stewart, 46, grew up in suburban Cleveland, Ohio.
Her father was a foreman at a factory and her mother was a homemaker.
Joan is the eldest of four children.

She attended Catholic schools, including a girls' high school,
then earned a bachelor's degree in journalism and political science.
Right after college Joan started as "cub reporter"
at a suburban newspaper, where she was quickly promoted to
city editor and later managing editor of a staff of 63.
Two years ago, after 22 years in newspapers, she founded her own
media relations consulting business.

Joan lives with her husband of nine years, Dave, and their three cats,
Speck, Cattin, and Fritz, in an old farmhouse in the country.

JOAN STEWART

Risk! Risk anything!
Care no more for the opinions of others,
for those voices. Do the hardest thing on earth for you.
Act for yourself. Face the truth.

KATHERINE MANSFIELD

MY MEMORIES OF BEING A LITTLE GIRL revolve around diapering my Tiny Tears doll. I emulated being a mom so I must have thought that someday I'd have my own live Tiny Tears to diaper, feed, and burp. I later graduated to Barbie, who in my play scenarios went to work and made money.

Both my parents were voracious newspaper readers, and we sat around the dinner table together every night talking about current events while we passed the roast beef. My parents were opinionated on everything from local politics to whatever was going on in far-flung places around the world. As a result I became opinionated myself and took a huge interest in what made the headlines.

Every afternoon at a quarter after four, the now-defunct *Cleveland Press* was delivered to our house. I would grab that newspaper, crouch on the floor on all fours, read every section, and look at the by-lines. To me the perfect life was to be a reporter working for the *Cleveland Press,* seeing my name in print, and being able to write about all that was happening in the world. I think I was born with the ability to express myself on the page, and I knew from a young age that that's what I wanted to do with my life.

Even before I got out of college I started to scheme ways to get into the *Cleveland Press.* I figured out that I could interview reporters there and write stories about them for my high school paper, and that's exactly what I did. The first person I interviewed was the society reporter who my mother always read and talked about: Beatrice Vincent. I will never forget what it was like to walk into the *Press* for the first time: It was a huge newsroom, filled with the fog of cigarette smoke, the clanging of typewriters, and the smell of newsprint. There was paper everywhere. Everyone was busy. I could feel my heart beating. I was in heaven! I watched everyone frantically running about, and I wanted to be one of them.

When I went to college, working on the school newspaper was as natural as slipping my foot into my most comfortable shoe. I became editor and covered all the seventies activism on campus. Once I graduated and got into the newspaper business, I made plans to get promoted, be an editor, meet lots of interesting people, and have my by-line at the top of page one. But I never made plans to have kids. The news business is tough and the hours are treacherous: I often sat in township trustee meetings until one o'clock in the morning, and I pulled many an all-nighter when I had four or five stories due the next day. I wasn't married then, so being single and not having kids allowed me to spend more time on the job than did my colleagues who were parents. And that was absolutely a good thing because reporting the news was my passion.

The newsroom was a male bastion for a long time, and I don't know of any women newspaper editors who were mothers yet managed to get ahead professionally. If I'd had kids I never would have achieved what I have in my career. I can remember my mom saying to my sisters and me, "Kids change your whole life. Kids become your life. And if you don't want kids to become your life, don't have kids." Most children would have taken this comment personally, but we knew it was just Mom being Mom—honest and opinionated. Before she died last year, my mom told me she thought I was wise not to have had kids.

In the mid-eighties, when I was thirty-three, I met Dave, who was also in the news business. Dave had moved around a lot, and I saw when I met him that kids were not his priority. He confirmed my observation, and I made it clear from the start that I was not interested in having kids either and that he needn't worry about me changing my mind. Dave and I are a good match: we each are extremely independent, and we each need a lot of personal space. We love our life together.

For most of my life, my mother struggled with one illness after another, and at age thirty-nine she was diagnosed with Parkinson's disease. I watched her shuffle as Parkinson's patients do, watched her shake and not be able to hold a glass of water in her hand, watched her finally confined to the house. At age forty-four my mother found herself pregnant, and she gave birth to my brother when I was sixteen.

Since Mom was sick, my beloved little brother became "my" baby. My two sisters and I took care of him, fed him, diapered him.

If I had an after-school activity, I'd go home after classes, pick him up, and take him back to school, where all the girls loved him and the nuns cooed over him. I got a lot of baby stuff out of my system with my brother.

I wasn't the only one in the house affected by watching Mom's life and listening to her comments about kids consuming your life. One sister and my brother also don't have kids, and that sister and I talk all the time about our choice not to have kids and joke that our cats are surrogates. My other sister, Lois, has two kids, so her desire for children must have been strong enough to outweigh Mom's influence. I watch Lois as a working mother, and I hear her say how tired she always feels. I wonder how she juggles everything.

I try to visit Lois and her kids a few times a year, and I've loved watching my niece and nephew grow up. I've spent many a Christmas Eve at Lois's house so I can be there when all the bedlam occurs. I love watching her and her husband haul the new bike up from the basement and wrap the last few gifts. I love putting the cookies and milk out for Santa. Things I haven't had a chance to do because I'm not a mom, I do at my sister's house. On those Christmas Eve nights I tell Lois, "When the kids get up in the morning, wake me! I want to be there!" She does, and I get to watch these little kids rip through their gifts and have a ball.

My relationship with Lois's two kids was great right from the start. I don't often get to hold a newborn baby, but when I held my niece and nephew I got that hit of what I call the "Johnson's Baby Powder smell" from their heads. When I smell that, I feel a couple of twinges in my stomach for a few seconds and ask myself, "Did I make a mistake by not having a baby?" The smell makes me want to touch the peach fuzz on the baby's "soft spot" or brush my finger across his cheek. Alas, behind every bundle of joy is a bundle of poop, and all it takes is a whiff of *that* to bring me back to earth.

I sometimes see the kids jump on Lois's lap, put their arms around her, and give her a big kiss and say, "Mommy, I love you." I will never know what that feels like, and at those moments I think about how different my life is and what I'm giving up to do what I do. Then I remember that that sweet moment between Lois and her kids may be great, but you can't have only that sweet moment— you've got to take the whole package. And I didn't want the whole package.

Sometimes I wonder, What would a child of mine be like? Would she beg me to read to her every night the way I begged my mom to read to me, or would she flout the curfew we set for her? Would he have Dave's bright blue eyes and love of animals, or would he run away from home and end up staring back at us from the side of a milk carton? The answers aren't easy even in the Land of Make Believe.

About two years ago I knew it was time to leave the newspaper business. I'd done everything I'd wanted to do and yearned for something different. I wanted to start my own business but the timing couldn't have been worse because Dave had decided to return to graduate school for a second master's degree. Nonetheless I took the plunge and started my own media relations consulting business. It has been the most frightening decision of my life and one of the most rewarding.

Going into business for myself has forced me to grow in ways I never imagined. I've learned how to be a contractor, bookkeeper, publisher, marketer, public speaker, strategic planner, and sole member of the office cleaning crew. I stopped buying sixty-dollar-a-jar face cream and learned the art of clipping coupons. The best part is that my business allows me to be more student than teacher, and being a student is where my growth and satisfaction come from. I want to continue down the road to see where it leads.

I feel about media relations consulting today the way I felt about newspaper work twenty years ago. In my networking activities I call people whose names I see in the newspaper and say to them, "You don't know me, but I just read about you in the paper, and you sound really interesting. Would you like to get together for coffee?" Usually they say yes, and we get together. With some I establish a relationship and with others I don't, but I benefit just from meeting and learning about them. At my core I'm a curious person, interested in people and what they do, what happens to them.

I used to have a mental checklist of what constituted the good life: a house, a husband, a set of Dansk dishes with all the serving pieces, and a job with good benefits, including a 401K plan that I could sock money into for retirement. And when I imagined myself at age sixty-five, I saw myself living the good retirement life, going out to lunch with friends a lot.

Two years ago, when I left my newspaper job, the checklist and the retirement vision changed radically. Today my list of re-quirements for the good life includes feeling the fear and doing it anyway, taking risks, taking complete responsibility for my own success, having a close circle of friends with whom I can grow spir-itually, giving back to the community through volunteer work, and knowing that I won't ever be left wondering about "what could have been" had I chickened out and not made good on my passion for starting a business. I imagine that I will not retire at sixty-five or maybe not even at seventy, simply because of how the economy is changing. If the cost of living keeps going up, I may be working at eighty! If so, I hope my business takes interesting twists and turns into uncharted territory.

I'm a bit afraid of growing old alone. When you see your friends' kids come home for Thanksgiving, you know that if their husbands die, they have their kids to take care of them, to spend Thanksgiving with them. I wonder about that. Yet I know I'm a person who won't let grass grow under my feet if I find myself alone at sixty-five or seventy-five. I'll make a phone call and say, "Hey, I saw your picture in the paper, and I think you look interesting. You want to spend Thanksgiving together?"

Princess Jackson-Smith, 53, grew up in Virginia.
Her mother taught music and her father was an attorney.
She has a younger brother.

Princess has worked as a community-development grants writer
and a parks department project director, and she is now
director of public affairs for a state-run transportation system.
She has a bachelor's degree in English.

Princess lives with Richard, her husband of 20 years.
She enjoys gardening, chamber music, ballroom dancing,
and reading. Her social life consists mainly of
entertaining at her casually elegant lakefront home and
involvement in community activities and organizations.

PRINCESS JACKSON-SMITH

> *Black, well read, busy:*
> *Spotted without small children,*
> *Lady bug wings it.*
>
> SANDRA E. JONES

COMING OF AGE DURING THE TURBULENT 1960s didn't have as great an impact on my childbearing decision as did my family background. I came from a revolutionary family, so we had always broken barriers, dealt with issues facing minorities, stood up for what we believed in. My early plan for my life was consistent with my upbringing, where first you get your degree—at least one—then you get married, then you have a baby.

At the end of the sixties I married, and my husband and I were ambivalent about children. We were civil rights activists, and he was a scholar, deeply involved in research. He was also a dependent person. I knew that when we married, but at age twenty-two I didn't know myself well enough to know that I wouldn't be able to carry that load. I'm not the mother type, able to be there for someone every minute over a long period of time. I can rise to any occasion in the name of love and devotion, but to be constantly needed is not something I can manage. We divorced—not because I didn't love him but because I couldn't manage the dependency load.

When I was single again I had many conversations with friends about our future prospects, and they were envisioning their lives as mothers. The only women I knew who were not imagining themselves raising children were women who couldn't get a date. So when it came to children I was the odd one. After the divorce I knew definitely that I didn't want a child, yet if I mentioned that to my friends, they'd say, "You'll change your mind."

I had to wrestle with the child issue because society expects that every woman will want to be a mother. Whatever else you're doing is fine, your career is fine, your desire to be the first woman in space is fine, but in addition—or perhaps first of all—society convinces you that you naturally have this built-in thing to want to be a mother. So my struggle was, What's wrong with me? Don't I feel it? *Don't I feel the built-in thing?* You don't want to come to grips with the fact that you don't feel the built-in thing because you think it makes you a freak. It's one thing to feel the urge and make an intellectual decision that your life can't accommodate motherhood. It's one thing if you haven't found the right man. But it's another not to feel the urge at all.

Nowadays when I see the lengths to which people go to conceive—fertility drugs, embryo implantations, surrogate motherhood— I think that urge must be unbelievably powerful. But it seems today that the urge is not just a desire to raise a child because if it were we'd see a lot more adoptions. No, the sperm must be his, the child must be biologically theirs. It used to be that when a couple had seen every doctor, and all the doctors had said that the couple was unlikely to conceive, that was the end of it; they arranged for adoption, devoted themselves to their nieces and nephews, or something. But now people say, "No! Get the petri dish! How many thousands is it going to cost?" I just shake my head.

I struggled with not feeling the urge to have a baby. I think many women must struggle as I did, because if you don't feel it you're going against all sorts of conscious and subconscious social, cultural, and familial messages. My parents had wanted a large family and had had only two children. They looked upon us as gifts, as blessings from God. And here I was, a girl with a happy life and devoted parents—how could I not feel whatever it is women were supposed to feel? It was hard to admit to myself that I didn't care at all about having children.

It took me a number of years to be comfortable with who I was, and fortunately my second marriage at age thirty was to Richard, who is older than I and not interested in reproduction. It also took me a while to realize that not everybody has the call to be a parent. People should stop and think about having children before they conceive. I'm so afraid of unprepared people, such as teenagers, having children without the necessary things being in place, without their understanding what it takes to be a good mother.

When people ask, "Do you have children?" I might say to them, "Help me to understand your need for this information." I hate to be rude but the question is rude. It's an icebreaker but it's intrusive. It's not that I have anything to hide, but why should children—whether or not you have them, and why you don't—be considered an appropriate topic for small talk? Suppose a woman is infertile and desperately wants children? How would this line of conversation make her feel?

Just because a woman doesn't have children doesn't mean she doesn't have to deal with family issues. Managers in workplaces today have to make it as easy as possible on employees, and so much of employees' stress levels revolve around their children. I regularly ask my staff members, "How is the soccer league? How are the clarinet lessons going?" because I want to understand their lives as parents. I send a Christmas gift and an Easter basket home with them for each of their children.

I encountered an interesting situation recently with a staff member who is married and has kids. One of her children caught chicken pox, so she was gone from the office for a week. My question to her was, "Couldn't your husband share some of this duty?" She explained to me, somewhat exasperatedly and somewhat indignantly, that when children are sick they want their mother and *no one else* — not their father, not their grandmother, and certainly not a sitter. I said, OK, I've learned something.

So many women in the work force today are single parents with no backup system. They have the pressure of the job, responsibilities at home, daycare calls when the child is sick, financial issues, balancing everything. I'm in awe of women who do this. It's hard enough with two parents, and yet many women are opting to do it alone. Some are trying to go to school on top of it all. My nerves would be shot! The people who baffle me are those with second families — who raise a child or set of children, then divorce and remarry and decide to do it all over again, knowing all they know from the first time around.

Not having had children has allowed me to arrange my life in a certain way, but if I care about my world then I still am responsible to society. I have time, energy, and financial leeway that lots of parents don't have, and I can share these with children in my community.

I belong to two black women's service organizations that focus on youth. I may not be the member who takes the kids on the field trip, but I contribute to our projects by writing press releases and fund-raising letters, arranging flowers for a tea. I believe we all should do what we can in the service of children. Children everywhere are in need of adult relationships beyond their parents, and those of us who are not parents should bring our influence and talents to bear. It can be as simple as just listening to a child.

Richard and I have a friend who is five years old. His mother is a single parent who travels on her job, so he stays with us from time to time. What makes this arrangement workable is that we can decide when to have him and for how long. We adore having him and we miss him when we haven't seen him for a while. But we know when his visits are going to happen and when they're going to end, and we can plan for them as we would for any other activity.

We can see how tired his mother is, and we sometimes invite him over just to give her a respite. She says things such as, "You can't imagine how great it is just to have a peaceful bath." And I think, a bath is a luxury? I'd be crazed! I'm not made that way. I could probably handle motherhood the Jackie Kennedy way, where a nanny deals with the children most of the day, and Richard and I play and read and do other things that we like to do. For me, the joys of being a mother would not compensate for being tied down, always having to be alert, and the fact that the responsibility never ends. I'm fifty, and I'm still my mother's baby!

My brother is forty and never married. Recently we discussed the possibility of his having children, and he does envision himself a father someday. I like to envision myself as Auntie Princess. It'll be Christian Dior diapers all the way.

I believe that all of us, mothers and nonmothers, are creating all the time. Creating means recognizing and making the most of whatever is evolving at a particular moment. We need discipline to recognize where our creativity is taking us at any given time, and we can develop that discipline by meditation, reading, and journaling.

I have many creative pastimes: I love to arrange flowers, and I have a two-year-old cutting garden that's coming along. I like taking classes, cracking the mystery of interesting things, and I'm currently taking a classical music appreciation class, which I've wanted to do for years. I recently took up golf and see that it is exercise that I can enjoy until I die.

I do a lot of public speaking, mainly in the areas of personal communication and self-development. I try to inspire people to pursue the type of life they want to have and be the person they want to be. I encourage them not to let the fact that they didn't have good role models or are afraid of failure stop them. My quest is to help people turn their energy towards managing their problems rather than exorcising their demons. I try to present issues in a way that makes sense and motivates people.

When I'm old I will still be involved in communications somehow, in the community, doing volunteer work. I want to continue gardening, and I'll still be interested in the arts, certainly in music. Possibly I will be on the stage. Probably by age seventy or so, I'll have realized that time is running out, and I'll get disciplined and write about having been a black woman in the span of time I've lived in.

I hope I have the finances to take care of myself as long as I live. But who is going to take care of me in my old age? To whom shall I leave my house, my property? When my mind goes, who deals with my affairs? These are concerns. They aren't reasons to have children, but one of the ancillary benefits of having children is that you don't usually have to look too far for answers to these questions. I guess this is motivation for staying on good terms with my relatives!

Sheila Hoffman, 47, grew up in Rhode Island. Her father owned a
laundry and dry-cleaning plant; her mother was a homemaker
and later worked as a hospital clerk. She has a younger brother.

Sheila earned a bachelor's degree in textiles and clothing.
After college she spent three years in Korea and
five years in Germany as a civilian employee of the U.S. Army,
running recreation centers for soldiers. When she returned to the
United States, she worked for the YMCA as a program director,
then consulted as a community events manager. Sheila now designs and
produces newsletters for nonprofit organizations.

She lives with Spencer, her husband of 10 years.
Her favorite activities include working on her computer, reading,
meditating, and exercise. Sheila is a longtime volunteer for
EarthSave International, a nonprofit organization that "promotes
food choices that are healthy for people and the planet."

SHEILA HOFFMAN

You might do a hundred things, but if you fail to do the one thing
for which you were sent, it will be as if you had done nothing.

RUMI

MY GRANDMOTHER DIED WHEN MY MOM WAS
seven years old, and that meant Mom had no role model for
what a traditional wife or mother was, so she could invent her
own style. Mom was always what other people might think of as
radical, since she marched and lobbied in favor of things she
believed in. She was a Girl Scout leader and also active in
Hadassah, a Jewish women's group. In many ways she modeled
an active life of service. Mom and I have always been close, and
if she influenced my choice not to have children, it was only that
she never encouraged me to have them. She enabled me to make
my own choices, and I always felt that I could be and do anything I wanted. If I had decided to become a parent, I could have
been a good one.

When I was growing up, in fact, I thought I wanted a lot of kids, and I imagined adopting children from all over the world. But because I was five years older than my brother, I spent quite a bit of time baby-sitting him as well as our next door neighbor's menopause child. Emotionally I have a sense of "been there, done that" when it comes to mothering. Yet today Spencer and I are designated guardians of my brother's children, and if something tragic happened to him and his wife, his kids would certainly have a home with us.

As a teen I was an introvert and slightly overweight. I had few close friends and didn't date. My mother used to dance with the USO during the war, and once when I was home from college and was bored, she suggested I go dance with the sailors at the Armed Forces YMCA. That night was life-changing! I had an incredible time, and when I went back to college I started arranging to bus girls from campus down to those dances. I didn't go from being an introvert to an extrovert overnight, but something about being involved with the Y changed me from a little fish in a big pond to a big fish in a little pond.

A few years later I became president of the service organization. My mentor at the Y became my role model, and I wanted to do what she was doing. The Y wouldn't hire me until I was twenty-five, and when I graduated, the two employment choices most similar to the one I wanted at the Y were working for U.S. Army recreation centers or the Red Cross, both overseas. I chose the former and went to work for them right after college.

That was the early seventies. The Vietnam War was going on, overpopulation was beginning to be discussed, and feminism was on the rise. And there was certainly the whole threat of nuclear war, with people wondering how they could bring kids into the world when the future was so uncertain. I remember Mom sending me the first issue of *Ms.* magazine when I was working in Korea. That was when I realized that other women out there were like me. I saw that we women have many choices, including the choice not to have children.

I was in my first long-term relationship with a man who professed to dislike children. (He's now married and has kids, so I assume his feelings about parenthood changed.) I was working for the Army, where the majority of people I saw were having too many children, with fathers away. These kids weren't well-behaved, and I was less and less inclined to be around them. I was also aware of the Zero Population Growth movement and sympathized with it. So it was fine with me that this boyfriend didn't want children, and I began to think I really didn't want any either. I had a career, I was happily running the show, making money, and traveling around the world.

When that relationship ended I was in my mid-thirties, living the single life and dating again but aware of getting older. By then I was even less drawn to motherhood, plus the medical thinking at the time said it was unsafe to have kids in your late thirties. I didn't want to meet the right man only to experience some biological clock explosion that would make me race to have a child with him too quickly—or worse yet, to wait for the relationship to mature and have a child when I was too old. I sure didn't want to be sixty with a kid graduating from high school. So I decided to have a tubal ligation.

I met Spencer when he worked for me as head of a children's summer program, and we started dating after his job ended. When we met I had already decided to have the tubal ligation, and I remember saying to him, "It's obvious that you love children. I don't want to have children but I do want a husband. I don't want to waste time dating someone who is not a potential husband. So if you want kids, we're not even a possible match, and let's not get started." That was our first conversation about dating! It turned out that he and his former wife had decided not to have kids, and he was happy to stay that way.

Spencer and I continuously re-create our relationship by setting goals together each year. Currently we're working to pay off our mortgage early so that we can go to Europe when he's eligible for a sabbatical. We also do a relationship review every year between Christmas and New Year's. We have a list of questions we ask each other, and we keep a journal of our answers. The relationship review is a special tradition for us and another way in which we try to live our values.

Women who've chosen not to have children don't have many good role models. As recently as when I was making my decision, people assumed that if you didn't have children, you physically couldn't have them or something was psychologically wrong with you. Today none of my friends have kids, so I don't experience myself as a minority. Our neighborhood is made up mostly of adults, and our lifestyle is considered normal here.

Occasionally I get the question, "Do you have kids?" When someone asks me that I say, "No I don't, but my husband has twenty-four of them." Spencer is an elementary school teacher and a volunteer at a camp for kids with cancer. He needs children in his life, and he has a greater impact and influence on more children in these ways than if he had one or two with me.

I used to think that people who have children have a built-in sense of who they are because they have a clear purpose in life—raising their children—and those of us who don't have children have to search for meaning in our lives. But today I believe that parents may still have to search; it's just that their search may be postponed by eighteen years or so as they attend to all the demands of family living. We who don't have children get to start exploring our purpose in life a lot sooner.

For me it's interesting to see what creations women who are childless give birth to in the world: art, organizations, ideas, and so on. I'm a graphic designer, so I'm creating all the time. But my life is not only about artistry; it's also about creating in a broader sense—the home I live in, how I spend my time, my relationship with Spencer, our friendships, building community.

My volunteering for EarthSave has felt like the most purposeful work and the biggest contribution of my life thus far. In 1989 Spencer and I heard John Robbins, the author of *Diet for a New America*, speak. His proposition is that if each of us cut back our meat consumption by ten percent, we could save enough grain in animal feed to end world hunger. As a budding environmentalist I went to his presentation never thinking it would change my life, but it did. We began eating a plant-based diet, and soon we knew we wanted to pass the word too—not only about the environmental but also the compassionate reason for changing how we eat.

After attending that presentation I volunteered to head a committee to organize an EarthSave booth for Earth Day. At the group's next meeting I was selected to lead the local chapter that I'd continue to nurture for five years. As a volunteer I produced a quarterly newsletter and a Web site, and as a part-time staff member I wrote an operations manual on how to run a local group, and I mentored other groups around the country. Now I'm mentoring the person who has taken over as head of my local group, and for the second year I'm organizing a food festival. I also chair the marketing committee of the national board of directors.

I found this organization at a time when I had been wanting to volunteer my skills and make a difference. I do other things for my community, such as giving blood regularly and participating in health studies. But with EarthSave I feel that I've had a big impact in an ongoing way.

In the height of my years as an organizer I used to joke that when I got old I would run programs for my local senior center. At this point I don't know if I'll actually do that, but I expect to be active physically and involved in the community. I imagine that Spencer and I may still be living in this same house thirty or forty years from now, and I'll spend time with friends, feel healthy, and lead a fulfilling life.

Lillian Comas-Díaz, 47, was born in Chicago. When she was six years old, her family returned to their native Puerto Rico, where Lillian lived until she was 22. Her mother was a nurse and her father worked in factories and later drove a taxi. She has a younger brother.

When she was in her early twenties, Lillian returned to the United States and earned a Ph.D. in clinical psychology. She was on the faculty at Yale University for six years, then worked for the Office of Ethnic and Minority Affairs of the American Psychological Association. She began her private practice as a clinical psychologist in 1986.

Lillian's husband of 14 years, Fred, is a doctor who specializes in brain–behavior connection, and together they founded the Transcultural Mental Health Institute in Washington, D.C. Through the institute they provide clinical services and consultation to people who have immigrated to the United States, people of color, and Americans who are returning to the United States after living abroad.

LILLIAN COMAS-DÍAZ

We are all here to be bright torches that light one another's way. . . .
We must find our own particular way of loving the world and put our
energy into it. Decide your way of loving, and you will be rewarded.

DR. BERNIE SIEGEL

BY THE TIME I WAS ABOUT SIX I KNEW THAT
I wanted to be a psychologist. I didn't have the word for it, of
course, but I knew when the other kids in first and second grade
came to me with their problems instead of to the teacher that I
had some particular abilities to help people. Having moved from
Chicago to Puerto Rico—such different places!—I could relate
to problems of not fitting in, of being an outsider.

I don't know what I did for those kids who approached me in
elementary school or what they saw in me. But they seemed to feel
good about what I said to them, and that's how I got interested in
counseling. Throughout school I was drawn to science and art, and
when I read about psychologists being both scientist and artist, that

seemed the perfect blend for me. After high school I headed to college with that as my career goal and never diverted from it.

I also knew from an early age that I wasn't interested in having children, and I remember searching for role models for that choice and paying attention to their lives. Several of my teachers fit the bill, as did two women in my family, second cousins who lived in San Juan and frequently visited us. Their lives looked happy to me. I also found childfree women in history and in novels who had done interesting and important things with their lives.

All of this showed me that women can do anything, and that although we cannot control many things in life, we can control whether we have children. I understand that some women feel that controlling reproduction is not an option, but for me—being born when I was and being blessed with access to education—it was.

My parents had a traditional Latino marriage—my mother was subservient and my father domineering—and today they still relate to each other that way. Although my relationship with my mother has always been good, when I was young I knew that I didn't want to be like her. Luckily my grandmothers were avant-garde and progressive in their thinking. They didn't feel women were inferior to men, they believed in equal rights, and I heard them talk about those things.

My father would have preferred his first child to be a son, but neither my younger brother nor I met Papi's expectations of girls and boys—I was smart and my brother was artistic. I think this frustrated my father, and it wasn't until we grew up that he accepted us for who we are. Even so, he was always proud of me and supported my being intelligent. Whereas my mother might say to me, "If you study hard, you can become a nurse or a secretary," my father always said, "You were born in Chicago, which means you can run for president of the United States." My mother was afraid of my dreams—she couldn't imagine my ambitions—but my father, although he was macho, supported my going out into the world.

When I was in my twenties and early thirties, my parents assumed I was postponing having kids. I had told my mother when I was growing up that I didn't want to have children, but she had said, "You'll change your mind." Her hope that I would lasted a long time, and so did her denial about the way the situation looked.

In Latino culture, people don't address sensitive or difficult matters directly but instead use indirect communication. Over the years my mother made comments such as, "Your friend so-and-so had a baby," or "My friend so-and-so is having a great time as a grandmother." Eventually I realized that my parents were getting anxious when they started fishing for information by telling me of acquaintances who were adopting children. So finally I said, "Listen, Fred and I are not having fertility problems. We've decided not to have kids." I feared their reaction would run along the lines of, "Are you rejecting us by not following our example?" But I told them I was not interested in having children because I wanted to do other things, and they accepted my decision.

Latino culture is child-centered, and most girls in that culture grow up thinking they will be mothers. My cousin Elba, for example, has two kids whom her mother cares for during the day. She is an example of how Puerto Rican women are expected not only to have kids but also to work and be active in the community. And many women do it very well. I, however, wanted to pursue a career, travel, and explore my creativity. Most important, I did not want to be traditional, and when a woman within the Latino culture has children, she's forced to be traditional.

In a third-world country it's not easy to move beyond the class you're born into. I grew up in a working-class family, and I wanted to become a scholar because I knew that was my ticket out. When I told my parents I wanted to be a scholar, they didn't know what I was talking about, and of course they didn't have the means to send me to college. But they said, "Whatever you want to try to do, fine." I knew I would have to figure out a way to make it happen by myself. I earned excellent grades and received scholarships to the University of Puerto Rico. When I came to the U.S. with a master's degree I worked as a psychologist, earned money, and studied English. I then was awarded scholarships for my Ph.D. program.

Professionally I've tried to address some of the paradoxes in Latino culture that affect women and what they perceive as their choices in life, including choices about motherhood. In particular, some beautiful paradoxes are provided by the Catholic Church, including the Madonna/whore syndrome. In Spanish it is called *marianismo/hembrismo,* with *marianismo* meaning "like the Virgin Mary" and *hembrismo* meaning female, strong, and self-directed. In this paradox, on one level the message is that sex is only for procreation, and on another the message is that sex is for enjoyment.

This mixed message confuses many Latinas. They fall into the trap of thinking they must be traditionally feminine and negate their assertive or ambitious side in order to be respectable. They think that if they affirm these other parts, then they are not a good mother, good wife, good daughter, or good woman.

In my other work with clients at the institute and with victims of torture whom I counsel *pro bono,* I'm able to contribute to society in a way that is extremely rewarding. I can't begin to describe how it feels to know you've helped somebody through counseling. It's magical. Because I enjoy it so much, it doesn't always feel like hard work, and I tend to check in with myself every day: Did I help enough today? If I died tonight, do I feel good about my life thus far?

I went through menopause early, at age forty-two, which is usual in my family. In typical academic and psychologist fashion, I had read many books on menopause and believed I was prepared for it. So it surprised me when I found myself mourning losing the potential to have children.

As a psychologist I use the term "mourning" to describe an experience that's not necessarily tearful or depressing but is a definite release. Before a woman reaches menopause, the decision not to have children can be a decision to defer or postpone motherhood, whereas at menopause it's a primal understanding that motherhood was not chosen. For me the decision not to have children had been purely intellectual, and with the onset of menopause it also became physical. I'm very in tune with my body, and I had new feelings that the experiences of pregnancy and birth would not happen, never. My release of that potential gave me a closure that felt peaceful. I feel lucky to be able to live out my nurturing side by being a psychologist and *re-parenting* the people I work with.

The future looks good to me. Not being mainstream American is helpful when it comes to aging, because in returning to Puerto Rico and being exposed to other cultures I see that women get better as they age. Elsewhere, elderly people are more valued and respected for their wisdom and what they have to offer. And in Europe, South America, and Latin America, women's sexuality and sensuality are not related to age. Women can be sexually viable into their fifties and sixties—they're not going on the cover of *Seventeen* magazine, but they are regarded like vintage wine. When a culture gives older women permission to be attractive and self-assured and vibrant, they are. It's not like in the U.S., where if you're forty you're considered over the hill. My friends and I talk regularly about our desire not to become absorbed by the American view of aging.

Today I'm trying to harmonize my life, trying to incorporate more solitude and quiet. I also exercise in the hope that I will not only grow old but that I'll feel good when I get there. (Illness can happen, of course, and we all do the best we can with what's given to us.) I used to study modern dance, and I want to get back into dancing. I have a photo of myself at about age five in a flamenco dancer's dress that my grandmother bought for me for my birthday—I was so proud of it!—so maybe I will study flamenco and see if it's in my genes.

As "Aunt Lillian" to Elba's two kids, who are eleven and thirteen, I get to act as occasional parent. I wish I could go to Puerto Rico and the kids could come to see me more frequently because I end up missing some things when I see them only two or three times a year. I think their mother has told them that I'm the smart one in the family—the one who writes the books and appears on TV—and they should view me as a model for achievement. Yet the kids and I have fun together. When I'm in Puerto Rico they take me all over the place, and when they come to see me I take them around. I love their visits, but I'm relieved when they leave because I'm not used to living with kids.

Fred is a middle-class WASP who spent time in Brazil when he was in high school, living for a year with a Brazilian family and going to school. His exposure to Latin culture is a big reason we're together and a force behind our institute. When we started to date, Fred was completing his medical residency, and we discovered that we felt the same about parenthood.

He and I are very close. We practice in the same offices, have lunch together every day, co-author articles, live together, play together. I always wanted a very intimate relationship, and I think that not having children has enhanced our marriage. A threesome is less intense than a twosome because intimate energy is dispersed among more people. Childfree couples disperse energy to significant people such as family and friends, but those people don't live with them.

In my observation, when a couple is raising kids, they often have to forget about each other and throw themselves into the children's world, and this means they take a hiatus from the marriage and its development. Marriages survive that, and when the kids are grown and gone, couples can rediscover themselves. But couples without kids don't have to suspend the development of the marriage. They can operate at a different level.

Fred and I love to travel, dine out, read, and collect art, particularly Latin American art. In our travels we always are looking at the work of artists, and my brother's paintings and sculpture are part of our collection. We want to establish a foundation so we can donate the collection to a small museum when we die. It's one of many projects Fred and I have together, and it will be one of our legacies.

We've been talking for the last ten years about where we want to spend our old age. We'd like to own a warm-weather place, maybe in Puerto Rico, and we're trying to figure out how to divide our life between two places. Being bicultural, I'm used to dividing, so that won't be hard for me.

We all hear stories about growing old that can frighten us, yet I find comfort in discussions Fred and I have with some of our closest friends. Among the many people we socialize with are four childfree couples who are around our age. We have known each other for years, and we talk about growing old, not having children to depend upon later, and our willingness to be in each other's lives—not living together but being there for each other. Today we stay in close touch, looking out for each other when there is a crisis or illness, calling often, bringing food over, and so on. We're like sisters and brothers to each other, and we're essentially creating a family to grow old with.

Pat Lunneborg, 62, grew up in Philadelphia.
Her father directed a research lab, and her mother was a teacher and
then a full-time homemaker. She has a younger sister.

Pat has a Ph.D. in psychology. She worked as a clinical psychologist for
the Veterans Administration, then taught at a major university
for 20 years before retiring in 1987. Since then she has published
four books, including Women Changing Work *and*
Abortion: A Positive Choice, *and has completed another on men who*
choose not to have children, tentatively titled Not To Be a Father?

Pat and Cliff, her husband of 36 years, live half the year
in London and half in the United States. At the top of the list of
activities Pat enjoys is her work. She also likes to travel and read.

PAT LUNNEBORG

No one objects to a woman being a good writer or sculptor or geneticist
if at the same time she manages to be a good wife, a good mother,
good-looking, good-tempered, well-groomed, and unaggressive.

LESLIE M. MCINTYRE

WHEN I WAS A CHILD I WAS ORIENTED TO
science and I wanted to be a medical missionary. I always had a
vision of the world as a huge scale—all these bad people on one
side and good people on the other—and I thought it was important to get on the good side and to do good in my life. Early on
I adopted quite liberal views that dismayed my father but I think
secretly tickled my mother. She was a loving, caring woman who
suffered from depression, and my father was a man with many
biases. Although I tried to take after my mother, I wanted most
to please my dad by doing well in school, and I did. I came to view
myself as a high achiever and didn't see any reason I couldn't go
all the way educationally.

After graduating from college I studied in Munich and met my first husband. We got married the following year, when I was twenty-three, and the marriage lasted two-and-a-half years. Luckily a few years later I found Cliff. When he and I married we didn't even talk about having children together—we were in graduate school, then getting our first jobs. We used birth control assiduously to make sure nothing happened, but we never really talked about having kids.

After we'd been married for eleven years I began to reflect on how long I'd been on the Pill, and at that point Cliff and I did discuss having kids. It was obvious to us both that we were totally uninterested in having children because we hadn't made a single move toward that idea in more than a decade. So we said to each other, let's get rid of the birth-control routine and not worry about it any longer. We knew vasectomy was less risky and a simpler procedure than a tubal ligation, so Cliff made an appointment and I accompanied him to the doctor's office.

During the procedure the doctor said to Cliff, "We're halfway through, Mr. Johnson," and Cliff said, "My name is not Johnson, it's Lunneborg." The doctor blanched, went next door to the adjoining office, and knocked on the door, calling out, "Hey, Bill, do you have a Mr. Johnson in there?" The answer was affirmative, so Cliff's doctor came back and shrugged the whole thing off with, "Not to worry. We're all here today for the same purpose!"

We emerged from the vasectomy laughing at that mix-up and also feeling satisfied personally. We felt relief, of course, about having no more contraceptive worries. But more important we felt something akin to pride: we had taken a step forward together by acting upon our recognition that we didn't want to have children.

There's an old saying: When two people get married, the wife wants the husband to change, the husband doesn't want the wife to change, and both are disappointed. Well, I never wanted Cliff to change. I've always thought he was great. And because we didn't have children, our relationship never got diluted. We never had to share each other or see each other change in ways that would have damaged what we've built together.

I've seen kids impact marriages more negatively than positively. I know couples who've become narrow and bitter because their kids didn't turn out the way they wanted, and as parents they feel guilty and angry. I've seen women turn into shrews when they had children, and so many of the men—usually the sole breadwinners, working sixty hours a week and worried to death about losing their jobs—seem to lose their ability to enjoy and marvel at the small things in life.

Cliff and I are academics. The proportion of women academics who have kids is small, because about the only way for a woman to be successful in academia is to be single or married without children. Some women academics manage to do it all, but if you are ambitious and want to succeed you can't let much interfere. When I was in my forties I took up running and would train regularly for marathons. My colleagues criticized me even for that, saying, "Why are you spending all those hours out on the trail when you could be doing research?"

Cliff still teaches part-time, and he helps students grow and develop. Would he still be doing that if he'd been worn down by the burden of supporting a family? Would he be fit and healthy and have been able to survive prostate surgery as well as he did a year ago? I doubt it. I think our mental and physical fitness is rejuvenated by the way we've chosen to live.

Cliff is at the core of my emotional life. In our retirement we have become somewhat isolated together, although he still has colleagues and friends on campus. Cliff and I no longer do research together, but we share a home office for working on our separate projects, and we're constantly interacting—fixing meals, going for walks, shopping. The down side of spending so much time together is that I've put all my eggs in one basket. Last year when I came close to losing Cliff to cancer, it was daunting. Either of us will need a lot of help when we lose the other one, but we know how to get counseling and support.

I loved teaching—Community Psychology and Career Development were my favorite courses—and I loved my students. For years I was the only undergraduate advisor for a thousand students, and I was interested in how their careers progressed. I believe I touched a lot of lives in twenty years on campus. Teaching also fulfilled my need to care for and nurture people, and it's a kind of generativity that's guaranteed: if you give birth to a child, you don't know what you're going to get, but if you're a good teacher, what you put into people usually sticks.

I feel I've also contributed to society through my books. My first book reviewed the literature on women police officers, and I'm thinking about updating that. The second was *Women Changing Work*, based on two hundred interviews with women in traditionally male jobs. My third book, on abortion, showed that although the experience might be traumatic or painful, for many women it is a positive decision. And my most recent book, about men who don't want to father children, was fascinating to write. Each time I take on a writing project I open myself to all kinds of new information and get a lot of pleasure out of the research.

I know that I will always write. Why wouldn't I, when it is a source of so much satisfaction? One day I'll write about the rehabilitation process after prostate surgery—there's a lot of misinformation out there, and I want to inform others about the alternative treatments that Cliff and I discovered after his surgery. Like that one, I'm sure all my writing topics will come from my life experiences.

I should hope that Cliff and I can hang on to our two homes in England and the U.S. We've remodeled one to include an apartment for a nurse or attendant to live in, and of course there is the nursing-home option in both countries if and when we need that. I don't see any reason why we can't go on living for many years as we do now, half the year in each place. I see it as a matter of shipping our bodies back and forth.

I hope that when we're old, we are well enough to continue to enjoy walking holidays. Three years ago we walked around Rome at Christmas for nine days, and after that the mountainous island of Madeira. Two years ago we explored the Egyptian pyramids, and last year we went to South Africa. There are Mediterranean cruises and all kinds of excursions for seniors that we don't yet take, and I can see us doing that years from now.

A long time ago Cliff and I were walking around a promontory in Cornwall. We met a very old couple working in a little tea shack out at the end. Here in this little room, these two people were shaking as they buttered the bread. He'd lose track of where he was and wander off, and she'd go get him and bring him back. As I watched this, I thought, Perfect! If nothing else, Cliff and I will help each other get through Sunday tea in a little shack at the end of the world.

Amy Sie, 52, grew up in Hong Kong, the daughter of ethnic-Chinese
parents who came to Hong Kong from Indonesia. Her father managed
the consular offices for the Indonesian government in Hong Kong and
later ran a shipping company and a factory. Her mother was a housewife
and later sold life insurance. Amy is the middle child of five;
an older sister died in infancy, and a younger brother died at eight of cancer.

When she was 20, Amy followed her best friend to attend college
in the United States, where she has remained, becoming a citizen in 1975.
She has a master's degree in social work, and her career
has included being a psychiatric social worker for a state juvenile
rehabilitation agency, therapist for young children in a day-treatment
program at a state hospital, and school social worker.
She is currently a social worker at an alternative high school.

Cerebral, introverted, Amy lives alone in a new suburban home
that is beautifully decorated with Indonesian and Chinese art.
She sings in a chorale, plays the baby grand piano in her living room,
and is an avid patron of the performing arts.

AMY YU-MEI SIE

If women truly see themselves as mothers,
then they can give pure, unconditional love to anyone.
This is what the world definitely requires today.

ASHA MA

AS A KID I WAS A PATIENT LISTENER AND A problem-solver, which helped me move easily among the different cliques at my school. At home things were quite different. I didn't get along with my father because I was outspoken and independent, which was unusual for a Chinese daughter. I never agreed with anything he said, and we were always at loggerheads.

My mother had left her home and family in Indonesia as a young woman to come to Hong Kong, ostensibly to study English but in part to escape an arranged marriage. She met and married my father, who was ten years older than she was and something of an authority figure. It seemed to me that she allowed him to dominate her, which caused me to lose respect for her when I was young. Much later in life, though, I began to appreciate various things about her—her brave move to Hong Kong, her success as a businesswoman.

If I had stayed in Hong Kong I probably would have gone to university and chosen a teaching career, gotten married, and had kids, as most females there did. But I wanted to do something different. I loved reading and wanted to pursue a library science degree. The University of Hong Kong didn't offer such a program, so I persuaded my father to let me go to the United States, to a college in Minnesota that my best friend had recommended, to pursue the degree. He told me that he would give me one-way airfare and one year's tuition and expenses, and that I would have to figure out the rest.

Coming to the U.S. for college seemed to open up a million opportunities. I got a scholarship the second year, and I took classes— including sociology and psychology—that would never have been available to me in Hong Kong. Those classes showed me that I could actually study relationships and do something professionally with my innate interest in them, and I eventually earned a master's degree in social work.

All my professional life I've focused on activities that support kids and their parents. In the days when I was a therapist for young, emotionally disturbed children who'd been admitted to a state hospital day-treatment program, schools didn't have social workers and didn't invite parents to get involved as they do today. So by the time I saw kids at the state hospital, it was almost too late to help them, and when they went back to their regular schools they had no support or monitoring. I became a big believer in prevention activities.

When I was a social worker in elementary schools, I initiated different kinds of prevention programs, each founded on the same principle: a good connection with an adult is a booster shot that helps at-risk kids ward off negative influences in the same way a booster shot can strengthen our physical body's immune system to ward off disease. At the alternative high school where I work today, I take a similar approach in trying to help teenagers succeed despite their emotional problems and difficult family lives.

When I worked in elementary schools I ran parenting classes. Some of the parents saw this as strange, given that I wasn't a mother, and they asked me, "How can you run a parents' group when you don't have kids?" When people ask questions like that, I'm not offended, because they're just curious, and I like to encourage curiosity. These parents were wondering how I could teach parenting, and that helped me to think about what I could offer, what I could give them. Because I'm not in the middle of their problems, I can often see situations more clearly. And because I get along well with young people, I can often serve as a translator or mediator for what's going on between them and their parents.

I've been in social work for nearly thirty years. The only way to survive in a field where you see so many bad things happen to kids is to have some distance and not get personally involved. If you get angry or depressed you cannot do the work and you're useless to the kids. I can't save everyone, but I do my best to give information and provide protection, and I don't interfere with other people's decisions. I'm an optimist and believe that things will usually turn out OK. That philosophy has helped me to last professionally.

I've had no children of my own, but in spirit I'm a mother. My job puts me right at the center of where kids spend their days, right in the heart of kids growing up, right at their service.

In my twenties I became deeply involved with a man who had older children from a former marriage, and he'd had a vasectomy. I knew this and didn't hesitate to commit to him, and I suppose that was my first realization that not bearing children was not a problem for me. This pattern repeated with men I was involved with later, one of whom I was married to for less than a year.

Turning forty forced me to see that decisions I'd made had ruled out having biological children and a traditional family. For a short time I toyed with the idea of adopting a child and being a single parent. I tend to think an idea through, bounce it off people who are my sounding boards, listen to their feedback, then either take action or not. In this case I talked to several close friends who reminded me that I was without a support network, and I saw that they were right. Adopting a child when I don't have a husband or support system wouldn't be good for me or a child.

I also saw that working with troubled families outweighed the fantasy of shaping a child into some ideal of what I would have liked to be. And I might have feared that no matter what I intended, I might raise a child like I was raised. My parents provided shelter and an education but were neglectful and not very involved in my life. If my approach weren't hands-off like theirs, it might have been the opposite—overinvolved and smothering.

After deciding not to adopt and the death of both parents, I was unencumbered by obligations. I focused all my energy into my work, resulting in ten years of the most productive and enriching experiences of my life. In 1991 I received a statewide honor when I was named "School Social Worker of the Year" by my colleagues.

Since deciding to remain childless, I have felt at various times anxious, exhilarated, and contented. My moments of anxiety come when—like everyone, including mothers—I think about the paths not taken. But most of the time I feel contented, especially when I listen to parents talk about their concerns for their children, their feelings of helplessness when things go wrong. I often go to court with kids who are out of control, refusing to follow directions, using drugs, sometimes prostituting themselves—kids whose parents feel like they've lost their child. I try to reassure the parents that things might change down the road and the child might come back. In those situations I think, "I'm so glad I don't have to go through this."

I feel satisfied with what I've become. I have an ever-growing confidence that I made the right choice, one that allows my personality to shine, that allows me to make my life meaningful and to contribute to the well-being of others. And in recent years I have concentrated more on my life outside of work, tasking risks in starting new relationships and redefining what my "family" looks like. I'm still plugging away at it and am surprised by all the different possibilities I feel comfortable with.

I have sung all my life, mostly in female choruses and church choirs, and for the last fourteen years I've been a member of a community chorale. Now I'm its president, and the friendships that have evolved from the chorale have resulted in "the cruise group," which vacations on cruise ships together. I absolutely love the performing arts and I hold season passes to two theater companies, the opera, and the symphony. I also love watching TV programming that's related to the arts, and anything educational—PBS, the Discovery Channel, A&E. A part of me is an introvert, happy to cocoon, to read and watch TV and occasionally socialize. Yet I think my life is probably richer than the lives of most people I know in that I have good friends who care about me, a comfortable home where I enjoy my privacy, and a job that puts me in contact with people and meets my needs for connection and involvement.

I'll be eligible to retire in three years, and my dream is to have time to do whatever I want to do in music and maybe to start my own clothing-design business, making clothes for women like me who are aging and can't fit into clothes labeled "petite." That would be completely different from what I've been doing, yet it would use the skills I've developed over so many years of working with people.

I don't think my life will change that much as I get older. I'll still be involved in the arts, possibly volunteering for the opera so I can go backstage and see what's going on. I like to travel but I don't like discomfort, and the places that I think would be most interesting to visit would require me to suffer a bit with mosquitoes and heat. I might satisfy my desire for some kinds of travel by watching travelogues on TV or video and seeing the world through others' eyes. I also wouldn't mind going on cruises that feature live classical music.

I've been careful financially and have saved for more than twenty years. I'll be better off when I retire than while I'm working! To have started investing so early I must have known that I would not have kids and would have to take care of myself. I'm allowing myself to think about all the possibilities that may be open to me after retirement; I love to brainstorm and explore, to pursue things that stimulate me. I'm very creative, and there's no shortage of ideas that are interesting and doable.

Christine Swanberg, 48, grew up in northern Illinois.
Her mother was a homemaker and her father was a high school business
teacher. She had a younger brother who died seven years ago at age 37.

Christine has a master's degree in English.
She taught high school English, speech, and drama for fifteen years,
then a decade ago moved to her current job as director
of communications and instructor at a private business college.
Over the last 18 years, Christine has published six books of poetry,
including her latest titles, The Tenderness of Memory *and*
Slow Miracle. *Her poetry has appeared in more than 40 magazines,*
and she has been anthologized in women's collections, most notably
I Am Becoming the Woman I've Wanted,
a 1995 American Book Award winner. She is working on her first novel.

Christine lives with Jeff, her husband of 25 years, and
two elderly cats, Spot and Mimsy, and a recently arrived stray, Maybe.
Their house is filled with Jeff's photography, travel mementos,
and family heirlooms.

CHRISTINE SWANBERG

True artists, true poets, generate and give birth today, tomorrow, ever.

HONORÉ DE BALZAC

THE FIRST SEVERAL YEARS OF MY LIFE WERE tranquil, as Mom and Dad and I lived in a cottage on a small lake while my father went to school. I've always yearned to get back to that simplicity—a peaceful setting near the water.

Naturally when you're the first child and a sibling comes along, it's unsettling. And my brother, who became profoundly retarded at sixteen months from encephalitis of the brain, demanded far more attention than a normal child would; until he turned twenty and was moved to the group home where he spent the rest of his life, one of my parents was always attending to him.

Yet I was not neglected in any way—I still had birthday parties and nice Christmases and all that—and even though my mother had to be there more for my brother than other mothers had to be for their children, she lived a life pretty similar to that of her friends.

From my point of view, that life was domestic toil spiced with a little TV, phone chats, and kaffeeklatsches. Though hers was a good and useful life, I didn't want to emulate it—I felt restless and adventure-some and destined for extending myself beyond the home.

At an early age I began to put energy into my life outside my family. I loved school and related really well to teachers. I was a vivacious and popular teenager, filling my life with friends and activities. Over the years I've reflected on how having a handi-capped brother affected who I became, and I think I would have turned out the way I did no matter who I had for a sibling: nature and words were my primary loves as a child and they still are today. But by baby-sitting my brother, whom I loved, and baby-sitting neighbor kids, I learned that I wasn't interested in caretaking oth-ers' physical needs. I don't want to be in charge of someone else's life all the time, and it felt natural for me to remain childfree.

The Romantic poet John Keats said that embracing the fact that not everything can be explained or reasoned creates enchant-ment and romance and the ability to experience life fully. In that spirit I refused to allow my brother's body to be autopsied when he died because he'd never been cut into. That was my way of saying, "I accept the mystery of all this." In some ways my brother's retar-dation forced me to learn lessons of acceptance faster than many people have to learn them. I learned early to accept what I am, what I'm not, and what I'm never going to be.

For my generation, roles for women were still limited to housewife, nurse, secretary, or teacher. In high school I thought about becoming a physical therapist or nurse, but working briefly in a hospital showed me that I could never flourish in that environment. Secretarial work held no appeal for me. Teachers were always my role models, and becoming a teacher felt like a good fit. When I think about the hundreds of people to whom I've taught language and literature, whom I've encouraged and nurtured, who have become writers or who have good jobs using what they learned in my classes, I feel like I've made a major contribution in twenty-five years of teaching.

At the small college where I've taught for the last ten years, so many women students in my classes have two or three kids, are not married, and have no support system. They're always kind of out of it—tired, foggy, stretched thin—and many of them work full-time and go to school full-time. I don't know how they do it. I can't imagine living without time, solitude, and serenity. When I'm done working I have to come home to a quiet house, not blaring radios and three TV sets on.

I teach the speech class, and every term at least half these women students will stand before the class and say, "I'm here to better myself for my kids." A part of me wants to say, "Why don't you just want to better yourself? Of course your kids will benefit from your efforts, but wouldn't it have occurred to you to do this if you didn't have kids?" I want to be sensitive to their identities and the choices they've made, so I try to remember that parenthood may be the thing that wakes some people up and supplies them with a purpose.

I first began to express myself in writing when I was a teenager by pouring my heart into original folk songs. And around age thirty I took a sabbatical to find out what kind of serious writer I could be. I took every writing class available at a nearby university— playwriting, fiction, poetry—and ended up earning a special degree in writing. My first book of poetry, *Tonight on This Late Road*, was published in 1984, two years after that sabbatical.

Teaching has supported my poetry and now fiction. Since I love to travel, I try to find a bookstore, cafe, or gallery in the area where

I'm vacationing that would like to schedule a poetry reading. I've read my work all over the country—and sometimes I even get paid for it! I've also judged several poetry contests. In my life, one event seems to lead to another.

Jeff and I didn't talk before we married about having kids. It was the time of Woodstock (which I went to, by the way) and life was free-flowing. I met Jeff, and a few months later we decided we wanted to travel, so we went to San Francisco for a few weeks. One day we were at a flea market and saw some beautiful rings. Jeff said, "Let's get the rings," then "Let's get married." We returned to Illinois and planned a wedding.

Occasionally throughout our late twenties and early thirties we'd mention the possibility of having kids, and we were ambivalent. I knew that relating intensely to a child all day would be confining, and the "great daycare shuffle" seemed too complicated. Finally one event—my best friend's baby shower—helped me realize my true feelings.

Jane and I had lived parallel lives since third grade—eventually exploring the same things in college and getting married at the same time—but when Jane neared age thirty, she became obsessed with wanting to have a child. She was unable to conceive, went through agonizing surgeries, received treatments abroad, and ultimately decided to adopt. Her baby shower was held in a dark house on a winter night, and I nearly suffocated in that room—all the games, the "How adorable!" comments made me feel like a foreigner. Physically I wanted to bolt, and I excused myself, saying I had to go. Outside, the cold night air felt so refreshing.

After that Jane continually told me I was "resisting" motherhood, and that ruined our friendship. I found it easy to let go of Jane because she expected me to validate her need to be a mother, which I did, but she could not validate my need to not be a mother.

One day a few months after the shower, Jeff and I were having a picnic, and I said, "If you really want kids, you have to tell me, because otherwise we're not having any." I honestly don't know what I would have done if he had said that he really wanted children because by then I was certain I did not. Fortunately he responded that he was happy without children too, and that was that.

For the first ten years of our marriage, Jeff and I were both teachers with summers off. Every February I'd propose, "Let's go to Turkey this year," or "Let's go to Guatemala," then that summer we'd go. Jeff and I traveled to Italy three times the adventuresome way—not having the trips all mapped out but instead saying, "Let's go here and see what we find." During those summers we went where the wind blew. It was glorious.

Today we're not jet-setters but neither are we like so many people we know whose vacations consist of camping sixty miles from home. We fly off for a week to somewhere beautiful and create short rituals of splendor for ourselves. These trips compensate us for not having summers off anymore, for not currently being able to spend large blocks of time in places we want to be, especially near the ocean. I feel so good when I'm next to the ocean that sometimes I think I'll go mad without it.

Jeff and I are directors at the same college. We also participate creatively in our church—this year I wrote the Lenten services, and Jeff took photos to illustrate them. Between living together for twenty-five years, sharing our religious faith, and traveling throughout the world, we've become soul mates.

Like John Lennon said, life is what happens when you're making other plans. We don't know what the future holds, but when I imagine it I see myself using my time and energy differently than I do now.

I'm passionate about music yet today I sing in the choir only four hours a week, so eventually I want to sing more in a large community chorus and regularly check out tons of music from the library.

I'm trying to create a better balance between career and other things I love to do. I now want to bring beauty and harmony to the world by sharing the more sublime gifts I've been given, such as singing and writing. Spending more time with music and writing means working less at the college. Earning less means not traveling several times a year — and if you've ever lived through a Midwestern winter, you know how strong the urge is to get out of it! I'm looking for the way to do what I want to do — sing and write — and still have enough money for travel.

My fantasy is to spend my final days on the Oregon coast, but when we're old we may need to be near family who care about us. As Robert Frost wrote, "Home is the place where, when you have to go there, they have to take you in."

Jeff and I have discussed one alternative to being with our families when we're old: a church-affiliated retirement home, where you give them a founder's fee and you live in a neat cottage until you become infirm. They take care of you until you die and even handle your funeral and estate. Several retired people I know who are parents have opted for that arrangement because their kids are spread out all over, and it's easier and more fun just to stay in a retirement village. I don't see people with kids as having many more alternatives in old age than those without kids. Having alternatives boils down to planning and money.

When I'm old, I'd love to sit on the ocean shore and eat Salerno butter cookies. I'm not kidding — cholesterol be damned! I imagine myself moving slowly and having a few people waiting on me a little bit. So what if I have to pay them?

Georgiana Arnold, 51, grew up in the Pacific Northwest.
Her parents separated when she was five years old,
her father died when she was 12, and her mother worked for an airplane
manufacturer. Georgiana is the eldest of five children.
An older sister died shortly after birth.

Georgiana has a master's degree in public health education,
has worked in health and social services for
most of her professional life, and currently directs a public health
project involving community groups and private institutions.
She lives in an urban condominium filled with art
and collectibles acquired during her trips to Africa, Europe,
South America, and the Caribbean.

GEORGIANA ARNOLD

*Wisdom comes from applying yourself wholeheartedly
to whatever you're doing. The lessons of life are in everything.*

PEMA CHÖDRÖN

MY FAMILY WAS POOR. WHEN MY PARENTS
separated, my mother was the sole support of a family of six, and
we lived in a housing project originally built for military families
during World War II. I felt safe in our multiracial neighborhood,
but that feeling disappeared whenever I ventured out into the
"real world." It's difficult to describe, but even at that age I realized there was a center and a margin, and I knew I lived on the
margin.

Movies and television offered a window to a broader, whiter
world, and at age seven or eight I fell in love with Hollywood's alternatives to my cultural and geographical isolation. I saw that my life
was a lesser version of what was on the big screen, and I quickly

realized that I didn't want to emulate the women in my world. In time I found a key to that bigger and better life: education.

I attended a Catholic girls' high school, and I was a good student and avid reader yet introverted and shy, with wobbly self-esteem. But I paid attention to women's lives that I saw in and out of school, and several times I had a searing realization, "Something's wrong with this picture." I remember noticing the energy that women generally devoted to getting and keeping men, and I questioned whether it was worth their time and effort. It also disturbed and offended me to realize that women can be perceived by men as replaceable objects or work mules. And my mother's life left me feeling conflicted at various points over the years because I saw her as too willing to set her dreams and desires aside for her children.

I said to her once, "Mom, when I look at what it takes to raise kids today, I see that it's tougher than it used to be; there are so many countervailing forces to a parent's word and example. One of the most life-affirming choices I ever made was not to have children. I'm so clear that this was the correct choice for me." And she replied, "I can understand why you feel that way."

Mother has been a tremendous source of support in my life: she wants me to be happy and is comfortable with my making choices out of the mainstream. I believe that she herself may have chosen not to marry or have children if those choices had been available to young women in her day.

The intellectual life—reading, studying, discussing ideas—has always attracted me. A lot of people want to be attached to other people, but my life is about attachment to people and to ideas. In the late sixties and seventies I was attracted to feminist writers such as bell hooks, Gloria Steinem, Simone de Beauvoir, and Alice

Walker, who raised so many questions about traditional female roles and challenged me to expand my thinking about the possibilities for my life. The civil rights movement, which was explosive during that time, also transformed me. I consumed the newscasts that described the trials, accomplishments, and courage of Martin Luther King, Jr., Malcolm X, and Stokely Carmichael.

In my twenties and thirties I took charge of my education and focused on reading and travel, taking my first extended trip to Europe when I was twenty-one. What an experience! I remember thinking, "Auntie Mame was right: 'Life is a banquet, and most poor sons of bitches are starving to death.'" That trip transformed my life and confirmed my identity as a citizen of the world.

In my late twenties I met my great love, my soul mate, and we were together for three years. He's the only man I ever considered having children with. He was a brilliant scholar, handsome, and truly devoted to me, but he also had serious emotional problems, and over time I realized that I had to let go of that relationship. As of today I haven't met another man who comes even close to his intelligence and spiritual beauty.

When I think about it, I see that a constellation of many things past and present—my family history, my education, my temperament and personality, my relationships, my certainty that I did not want to be a single mother—influenced my decision not to have children, and that decision has allowed me to pour most of my time and energy into work. By training and inclination I'm an educator—I *love* to teach, and it's one of my strongest gifts. Volunteer work has always been a large part of my life too, and I've worked as a volunteer on health-care access and reform, diversity and women's issues, and public health programs.

When I was in my thirties I didn't understand that my life has an internal ribbon of meaning that is always there, even if I'm not aware of it at the moment. Although today I sometimes still have questions about the true purpose of my time on earth, I'm clear that part of living is having faith. Women who consider not having children may fear they won't have love in their lives, but love is all around us! We are the ones who insist on a certain packaging and presentation—if it's love, it's got to come in this skin color, this age, this setting—when, in fact, love is always available if we're willing to release our preconceptions. Learning to embrace my life and let it flow has been a key to happiness for me.

I don't understand people who can't see how hard parenting is. I want to shake them and say, "Don't you have eyes? Can't you see the concentrated time, maturity, social skills, and teaching ability required to raise healthy children?" Not everybody is suited to the job, but most women are able to assist in parenting as aunts and godmothers if they choose. I'm satisfied playing those roles.

We who don't have children often have more time and money than our parenting siblings and friends, so we can play integral roles in their families—not only giving parents a needed break but also providing financial and other resources for their children. There's always been a large cadre of well-educated, single women in the African-American community and a tradition of these women providing leadership, resources, and expertise in various ways. There's also a strong tradition of single, childless women having good interactions with children through their friends and families.

Children are such a gift to me now. I didn't feel that way in my twenties and thirties because I was preoccupied with other things. Today I try to let all the children in my life know how special they are to me. Interactions with kids don't have to be a big deal. Sometimes I just send a card to one of my small friends. Children love to receive mail, love to know you're thinking about them. I have a pen pal whom I met when she was eleven years old, and this past June she graduated from high school. We've kept up our correspondence, and I've been another adult voice in her life.

Children also love to have relationships with adults that don't entail discipline. And single parents need friends who can be buffers when they're exhausted or at wits' end, someone to say, "I'm going to take the kids for the weekend. Don't worry about them." When I was growing up, sometimes my mother needed that break, and there were a few women who would take us children for a couple of weeks at a time. I think this is a great gift to give parents and children, and of all the contributions I make to family and friends, this one requires the most discipline because it takes the most time.

I've worked with schoolchildren on several occasions, and I see significant levels of depression among them, which is scary. Some are spaced out for the first two hours of the day; others are just plain neglected, and they're "limping." I've also worked with children who are loved and nurtured, and they believe that they can conquer the world—they're present, energetic, and healthy.

I'm convinced that if we just paid attention to the children who are already on the planet, we'd have our hands full. Everybody does not need to have his or her own kids to nurture. There are so many opportunities to care for children in ways that are loving to them and respectful of our own skill levels.

I'm not worried about growing old alone because in my family we're going to have each other. My family contains several young children, and it's tempting to do things with them as a group, but if I do this too often I'll never get to know them as individuals. So we also take individual outings to the movies, children's museum, or restaurants. Sometimes we just hang out. As I grow older I want to spend more time with them.

Cary Grant was my movie idol. The man was gorgeous and healthy until the day he died. When he passed away, I thought, "That's what I want—to be healthy until I die." I want to stay in love with all there is to experience and to know about life. At heart I'm a spiritual wanderer and adventurer, and I want to retain that sense of anticipation and excitement.

Vicki Heppner, 46, grew up in Washington State.
Her father was an electrician and a car salesman, and
her mother was a secretary and a sales clerk. Her parents divorced
when she was in her early teens, and both remarried.
Vicki has one brother, two sisters, and several stepbrothers.

Vicki married right after high school. In her thirties she earned
a bachelor's degree in industrial engineering, and in her early forties,
an MBA in finance. Today Vicki is the controller at an industrial firm
and also has a part-time, home-based accounting business. She lives in
a lakeside home with her husband, Mike, and her sister-in-law.

During her early teens, Vicki contracted rheumatic fever
and also was treated for arthritis. By her late teens, doctors changed
their diagnosis to lupus, and Vicki has been hospitalized
nearly a dozen times over the last 26 years for lupus-related illnesses.
Today she feels healthy and is active in community theater,
both as an actress and board member for a theater company.
She likes to read, dance, play piano, swim, fish, and golf.

VICKI HEPPNER

It is in the knowledge of the genuine conditions of our lives that we
must draw our strength to live and our reasons for living.

SIMONE DE BEAUVOIR

WHEN I WAS YOUNG I WANTED TO BE A
movie star. I never had any doubt about my ambition. That drive
stayed constant through high school when I was in plays and
made it to state drama competitions. If I could have afforded college, I would have studied acting. Just as high school was ending
I met Mike. Stardom had been my goal, and meeting him threw
me. But I fell instantly and completely in love.

As we were making plans to marry, I knew the marriage wouldn't
survive if I went for stardom and everything it would entail—moving,
working strange hours, interacting with Hollywood types. Mike
would have come second all the time, and I couldn't imagine that.
So I put off acting until ten years ago, and when I took it up again,
I was reborn. This time I took acting classes not to chase the star

but just because I wanted to, and I fell right back into my element. I still love to be on the stage.

When Mike and I were dating we talked about everything. I remember us lying on the floor of my living room and talking about having children. I asked him, How many children do you see yourself having? What do you think that would be like? I'd always thought I'd have two kids because my younger sister was so important to me, and Mike liked that number also. We went into marriage thinking we'd have two kids.

Soon after we married, both our sisters had babies. Mike and I were good with the two boys when they were little, and when they grew old enough, we took them on many weekend camping and fishing trips. Giving my sister and sister-in-law that relief certainly improved my relationship with them!

Yet spending time with my nephews never led me to feel a baby itch. In part that was because in addition to having fun with the kids, Mike and I recognized our joy in returning them to their parents. We liked to take them to McDonald's, but we also liked to go to a nice restaurant by ourselves for dinner. We noticed that none of our friends who were parents could afford to go out or could get a baby-sitter, a fact that made us rethink having kids. It helped us see that we didn't want to be parents twenty-four hours a day.

After we'd been married for about five years, I began to feel certain that I didn't want children. Off and on for six months, Mike and I had serious conversations in which I communicated my feelings, and by then Mike pretty much felt the same. I'd also seen that Mike and I have different viewpoints on child rearing because we come from such different family backgrounds. I believe kids should earn money through after-school jobs, for example, and he believes parents should give money to their kids to go on dates and such. My mom and stepdad fought a lot over children and money, and I saw how different philosophies can cause conflict in child rearing. How we raise children is based on how our parents raised us, and I knew that bringing up kids together would have been tough for Mike and me and might have destroyed our marriage. In a family if you don't have the marriage, you don't have anything.

I saw that my relationship with Mike, the person I love most in the world, was the high price I would pay for our having a child together, and it wasn't worth that cost to me. What's more, my doctor had advised me about the probability of miscarriage for lupus patients. I remember thinking, "Why would I want to go through that?" We decided to formalize our decision, and Mike agreed to have a vasectomy.

From the time we married through my mid-thirties, Mike and I got some strange reactions to our not having children. People assumed that we'd gotten married when I was so young because I was pregnant. Then after we'd been married a few years and I wasn't pregnant, people assumed there was something wrong with us, that we had physical or emotional problems.

That's the kind of experience we have at high school reunions, which are the pits. People pull out pictures of their kids—or now, their grandkids—and we say we don't have any children, and they don't know where to go from there. It's natural that kids are a big part of the conversation when parents are in the majority. But many parents are so caught up in that aspect of their life that it doesn't occur to them that they might ask about people's work or hobbies or anything else.

Mom and Dad were both drinkers, Dad had affairs, Mom always took him back after he caroused, and I always felt she did so because of us kids. There might have been a time in those early years when I looked at her experience and thought, "I will never be that vulnerable. I will never be in a position where I can't say, 'I'm outta here.'" That's probably the main thing, along with my disposition to work, that influenced my thinking about having children.

Mike and I come from alcoholic families filled with divorces and remarriages and divorces and remarriages. There's no core family, only one so fractured that it was impossible to have Christmas together. I can imagine planning a christening—"Let's invite Gramma, Gramma, and Gramma, and Grandpa, Grandpa, and Grandpa, but you can't have wine there, because so-and-so will overdo, and this gramma can't be around that grandpa because they hate each other since the divorce . . . "

It would have been hard to justify bringing children into a family with such a history of alcoholism. Plus, as I've said, I didn't think our marriage would survive with children, and I didn't want to make another fractured unit. My marriage to Mike was my priority, and ours is the only marriage in our families that has lasted.

My sisters and various friends whose children are grown tell me they would rethink their decision to have kids if they had it to do over. They love their kids yet realize how much time and money and effort it takes to have a child, especially for a single or divorced woman. Even if there are two parents and they both work, it takes everything they've got to make ends meet.

In hindsight these women wish for a lot of things—a career, more education, more intimacy with their husbands, the chance to be financially ahead. I don't think they are saying they chose the wrong avenue; I think they're wondering what they would have done with their own lives had they not been focusing on other lives all those years.

I'm so glad I decided not to have children. As I age I'm becoming "bigger," and I want to learn more, be more, contribute more. When women have children, their own lives are put on hold, and they lose so many years—at least ten to twenty, depending on how many kids they have. That's half my life! I don't believe any woman can be or have it all. I'm a high achiever so I'd want to be the very best mom, and although I believe I would have treated children of my own well, I think I would have resented them for the loss of myself.

Mike and I will semi-retire when I'm fifty, and even then I plan on being busy. We'll work part of the year and take off large chunks of time to play golf and have fun. We're designing a one-story retirement home for ourselves, complete with a dance floor and computer area.

Looking toward that time, I just began a two-year course at a theater conservatory. Describing what it's like for me to be on stage is like trying to describe savoring a luscious flavor—all I can say is that studying acting balances me and gives me my next set of goals. After I retire I may do commercials and voice-overs, or maybe develop a musical act. I also want to write a novel and take art classes.

My mom always asks, "Who's going to take care of you when you're old?" I live the life I do because I don't think I'll live long enough to get old. I don't see myself making it even to age sixty-eight for our fiftieth wedding anniversary; I don't think my lupus will allow it. For a long time I've imagined making it to age sixty, maybe, and that has influenced everything I've done. That's why I'm accelerating my retirement, why my life is always full, why I seek things out, why things come to me.

I've always been drawn to active people who lead full lives, who have things going on, things they can show me, like photos or music or art. In the same way, I expect people will seek me out as I get older because I always have a lot going on. For that reason I don't worry about not having kids to care for me later. There are no guarantees about that anyway. I have a great relationship with my two nephews—they're grown up now, but we still see each other often and enjoy each other's company.

Eventually my disease will prevent physical activities, and that's when I'll be painting and writing. I can tell you something else about those last years: My days will not drag, and I will always keep my relationship with Mike fresh. I love my life and wouldn't change anything about it, even my illness. It's helped make me who I am.

When I was young I thought, "I want to be great, to be recognized, to accomplish something big." Later I thought I wanted to change things in the social order. Now I see how little it takes to make an impact on someone's life because little things done or said by strangers have made big impressions on me. In other words, maybe it's not what we do but the lives we affect that makes a difference, and we all affect others' lives every day in ways we're often unaware of. My father and I reconnected before he died, touching each other's lives deeply, and my life has been influenced by a few children and many strangers. Having children so that there is something to follow you on earth? I don't think so. I believe you can touch people's lives, and *that's* what follows you on earth.

*Sarah Klein, 26, was adopted as an infant and
raised in upstate New York. Her mother is a speech pathologist
and her father was a teacher and now is a hotel manager.
Her parents divorced when Sarah was four and each has remarried.
She has a younger brother and several half- and step-siblings.*

*Sarah has bachelor's and master's degrees in China studies.
She currently teaches second grade at an inner-city school and coaches
swimming. She lives with her boyfriend, Keith.*

*Sarah enjoys the outdoors by hiking, camping, and swimming.
She also loves music, plays trumpet, and spends time
with friends and acquaintances.*

SARAH KLEIN

Develop interest in life as you see it,
in people, things, literature, music—the world is so rich,
simply throbbing with rich treasures, beautiful souls,
and interesting people.

HENRY MILLER

AFTER MY PARENTS DIVORCED, MY DAD MOVED and my brother and I saw him only on major holidays. Dad enjoyed us when we were young, which showed me that kids can be a pleasure. My mom became a survivor personality; her attitude about having my brother and me was probably joyous initially, but as we got older all the responsibilities for our upbringing buried that elation.

Motherhood seemed like such an enormous load—without many rewards—that I never desired it. I've told Mom that I don't plan to have kids. I can tell she doesn't necessarily approve of that choice but won't say she disapproves either. The thought of not having grandkids through me is probably hard to accept, but I think she's resigned to it.

There was never much to do in the small town where I grew up. My family didn't have a TV so I read voraciously for entertainment, and through reading I developed an interest in languages and cultures. By eighth grade I was studying French. When I was finishing high school, a family friend recommended I learn Chinese, and that sounded interesting. In college I focused on Asian studies, and my family was quick to give me suggestions about careers in international politics or economics.

People in my hometown had definite social rules about having children: they frowned upon young single mothers, and they noticed and discussed married couples who didn't have kids. But in the urban areas where I've lived the last several years, people are less personal, and the possibility of finding people who've made choices similar to mine is greater. I don't go back to my hometown often because life has taken me in a different direction, and I have less and less in common with the people I grew up with.

I've been a swim coach for years, and parents always say to me, "You're so good with kids!" I'm flattered by those remarks. These people often ask if I'm planning to have kids of my own. When I tell them no, sometimes their reaction *looks* like, "Give me back my kid!" yet they'll *say* something like, "Oh, but you're such a natural with children . . . "

When other people learn I don't intend to have kids, their responses are predictable: "Wait till you meet Mr. Right," or "Wait till your biological clock starts ticking." Many people consider having children to be the ultimate goal, and no one acknowledges that not having kids is a fine option that some women choose. It's hard to say for certain how I know at my age that I'll never want to have children. How does anybody know what they know about themselves? When it comes to big decisions I've always gone with my gut, and it never fails me. I know I want control of my life, and I think most women lose control over their lives when they have a child.

I remember in the early eighties seeing movies such as *Baby Boom* that tried to portray "liberated" women's roles — in that movie's case, the woman who could have a baby and also run a business. On TV the *thirtysomething* show had mothers going off to work in their tweed suits. And *Good Housekeeping* and *McCall's* magazines, which Mom subscribed to, ran articles like "Ten ways to cook dinner in five minutes" and "How to stitch your children's clothes while you're commuting."

My mom was a working mom, and I knew even then that all this was such crap! These movie and TV representations were so shallow, telling women they could have it all, selling such an unrealistic picture of what's possible. And then when women try to have careers and be parents, they don't get the backing of government programs, the companies they work for, or, in many cases, the Mr. Rights in their lives.

On our first date, Keith and I went to a hockey game, then to dinner, where we spent five hours talking. Since then things have moved fast between us but not unnaturally so. We're laying down a good foundation with dialogue and trust. We're giving ourselves the time to understand each other.

Importantly, Keith doesn't want children. For four years he's been a professional nanny to two kids, and he's seen what it's like to live in such a household. We've talked about marriage and children, and we agree that by not having kids, a couple can enjoy each other in ways they never could if they are parents. Keith says he's never wanted a marriage that revolved around or was filtered through children, and when we talk about getting married he says he's willing to have a vasectomy.

My criteria for a husband include his being willing to live a lifestyle that complements mine. He needs to be intellectually stimulating without being stuffy. He needs to be my best friend, of course. And it's important for us to be like-minded about not having children. Having a successful relationship can be hard enough; adding a baby would make it incredibly hard. Who plays what role? Often the man may want kids, but the woman has the kids, and she usually ends up taking care of the kids. It's like the dog scenario with a kid: the kid wants a dog, the parents buy the kid a dog, the parents take care of the dog.

My models for an ideal relationship are my godparents, Aunt Kay and Uncle Herb, who are childless and have been involved in my life since the moment I was brought home. They do a lot together and take an interest in others. They've stayed together and worked things out in their marriage. They really know each other and have all the space in the world to do that.

When I was finishing graduate school I thought I might want to teach in a minority setting. I've always been interested in race relations: I grew up near the Awkwasasne Reservation in upstate New York and was aware of the racial tensions between the whites and the Native Americans in our area, and when I first went to China in 1992 I was surprised by the overt racism there. In China white Americans and Europeans are considered different yet are welcomed, but other visitors—as well as China's own minorities—are disrespected and often hassled.

When I returned from China I began to discuss racial inequities in the U.S. with friends and fellow students. I read all of Jonathan Kozol's books and was struck in particular by *Savage Inequalities*. His work became a bridge that showed me how I could act on my feelings about racial and social injustice. Then a friend told me about the federal government's Teach for America program. I interviewed, they offered me a job, and I figured I could teach while making connections to get into international business, where I could use my China studies degree.

Today I know that at least for now I'm meant to teach underprivileged kids because it helps me fulfill my goals about breaking down stereotypes and challenging people to think about what we're doing with our educational system. Racial issues are tied to education, and I feel passionate about how this affects kids.

I teach second grade in one of the toughest urban areas of the country, where drug addiction and shootings are a way of life. My kids generally come from homes headed by poor single moms, and their test scores are among the lowest in the nation. The biggest problem in my classroom has been hitting and fighting, and I've tried to teach my students how to follow rules and resolve conflicts peacefully. I have tried to keep control of my class, be consistent and objective, have high expectations, and model respect for my students. In contrast to the beginning of the year, my kids are now the best behaved in our school. They line up to come in from recess, and they're quiet when they're asked to be.

In many ways teachers are an in-class mom to thirty students for eight hours a day. I get hugs and Mother's Day cards from my students. Some of them slip and call me "Mom" in the classroom. All this is nice, yet I can't imagine how women come home after a day of teaching and do the same thing with their own kids. For me that would be like giving up everything to the identity of "mom."

As it stands, when I get home from teaching I'm free to do what I want—spend time with Keith, practice Chinese, go to Irish step-dancing class with friends. I was free to pursue my master's degree quickly and be mobile in job-hunting, and I'm still free to pursue any satisfying career.

I've always felt that I had a lot of promise, that I could achieve what I want and do a lot with my life, and that's probably the biggest factor in my choice not to have kids. In the next ten years I'd like to go abroad and teach, then return to the U.S. and perhaps earn a Ph.D. in education, moving into administration and policy analysis.

My decision not to have children has been an evolving and emotional one, and sometimes I've questioned it, especially since I'm still young and capable of starting a family. But for me, having a child would mean putting a lot of other goals on hold, and a child would change my entire identity forever. Change and personal growth is an integral part of life, but I feel that my choice to grow in another direction will ultimately feel more fulfilling than mother-hood. I want to be a part of young peoples' lives in some way, and I expect to feel much more satisfied by reaching out to those already in the world and in need of someone who believes in them. I couldn't do that and give children of my own everything they would need as well. I've had to realize that as energetic as I am, I have limits.

It's hard to imagine old age from where I am now, but I know I'll want to stay active and live independently. I used to coach swimming at a health club that offered water aerobics classes for women and men who were pushing eighty. These people came three times a week and worked out, then went to have coffee or for a walk together. They were living active, social lives. I'm happy in my life today, and I aspire to that kind of life fifty or sixty years from now.

Sutapa Basu, 42, grew up in Calcutta, India.
Her mother was a homemaker and her father was a banker.
She has two older brothers.

Sutapa attended an English boarding school in India,
then came to the United States in 1975 to attend college.
She has worked as a sexual-assault prevention educator and
has directed women's centers at community colleges.
She is currently director of the women's center at a major university
and is finishing her Ph.D. in human and organizational development.

She lives with Jim, her partner of four years, and Kitty, their cat.
Jim has a grown daughter from a previous marriage.
Sutapa is involved in local politics, and her favorite activities include
reading, walking, traveling, and entertaining friends.

SUTAPA BASU

To this day I believe we are here on earth to live, grow, and do what we can to make this world a better place for all people to enjoy freedom.

ROSA PARKS

MY PARENTS CAME TO INDIA AS REFUGEES from what is now Bangladesh. At the time, India was under British colonial rule, and there was no local education for villagers, so the very wealthy sent their children to schools in England. My parents were poor because they had left their land and possessions behind, but my father managed to get an education later in life and subsequently worked hard and did well professionally. As a result he strongly emphasized education for all his children. Even though most Indian families invested in their sons, my father expected me to become a doctor as well as a homemaker, and he sent me to boarding school.

On the boarding school grounds, there was a little pond I liked to sit by. Once when I was at the pond I met the gardener and started to talk to him. Students were not permitted to talk to any of the help, but I talked with him that day and from time to time afterwards. He had left his village as a migrant worker, and one time he spoke of his two sons and his daughter, how he sent his wages back to his family so his sons could go to school. I wished that his daughter could go to school too, so I gave him my pocket money for two or three years for her education.

Because this was a strict school, I knew that if I got caught doing this I would get in trouble. Sure enough one day I was caught and punished and told never to speak to him again. My fear was not for myself but for him, that he would get fired, but he didn't. I still send money regularly to India to pay for the education of several girls there. I hope that eventually they get good jobs and do the same to help girls after them.

I was a good student, and my father promised that I could go to America to continue my education if I got a full undergraduate scholarship. But my father was afraid of losing me because people told him, "Don't send your daughter to America, especially unmarried. You'll never see her again." Several thousand people applied for the same scholarship I did, and my father didn't think I would get it. Only three recipients were chosen, and I was one of them. When I won, my father flew my brother Ashim, who was studying for his Ph.D. in the U.S., back to India to promise my father, face to face, that he would take care of me when I came to America.

At that time it was highly unusual for an Indian woman to be sent abroad without being married, and before I left, my father tried to get me married. Arranged marriages, where your parents pick the man you will marry, are still very popular in India. My parents found a man who had received a scholarship to Harvard, and my father thought he and I would be a good match. In line with tradition, the young man's parents came to see me, and his mother liked me so much that she started talking to me as if I were already her daughter-in-law. She said, "Oh, we have such a good friend-ship! I never had a daughter, and I cannot wait to spend time with you. In the afternoons you can massage my feet, and I will tell you stories."

My face must have contorted when she said that because my parents looked at me and knew instantly how I felt about massaging some mother-in-law's feet, which is still a common practice for many women in India. I was very polite, and as soon as she left I said to my parents, "If you think I'm going to consider marrying into that family, you are out of your minds." I had an independent streak in me, and this experience brought it out! My father made a few more unsuccessful attempts to get me married, and then I left for the U.S.

In college I chose to study social sciences rather than medicine. I got involved in diversity issues and became a budding activist my first year in the U.S. I had grown up in a country that exerts huge pressure on women to conform socially and in a strict boarding school with tremendous pressure to succeed academically, so it felt very different to meet people on my campus and get involved in social issues. Political activism became an important part of my life. That's when I became my own person.

The idea had been that after I finished my education I would go back to India and marry an Indian man, but I fell in love with and married the son of my host family in America. Before he and I married, we lived together for eight years without telling my parents. Finally I told them of my love for him and that we wanted to marry. We were married in India, and the marriage lasted seven years.

Even though I was involved in the women's movement in the U.S. and believed strongly in reproductive rights, I never thought that I myself had the option to not have children. I had grown up believing I would definitely have a family because in India a woman's worth is measured by her ability to have children—and that worth increases if she has a male child. I haven't met anyone yet in India who thinks she has a choice about whether or not to have a child. It's not a thought that women there—even educated women—would entertain.

I remember the exact moment I realized I had the same choice that Western women have regarding whether to become a mother. I was still a student and was driving home from campus, the only car on the freeway at two o'clock in the morning. It suddenly hit me: "I don't have to have children if I don't want to." Nothing in particular that I saw or heard right then prompted the thought, so it must have been brewing for a while. But it was incredible! Part of me felt really free, and part was totally scared.

I have saved the page from my diary where I recorded those thoughts the following day. But about two years passed before I digested the idea that I really had a choice. Over those two years I moved from "I don't have to have children" to "I don't want to have children," and that frightened me. From conversations we had, I knew my husband could go either way regarding children, but how would I explain my decision to my family and friends?

For a long time I didn't tell anyone. But at some point I thought, "OK, I must talk to people about this." On my next trip to India I told my friends. They thought I was lying, that I couldn't physically have children but wouldn't admit it. When I convinced them that wasn't the case, they said, "Why not have just one child?" These are progressive, professional women, and they didn't get it. I said, "I don't want children, but if I change my mind someday then I will adopt." Adopting is not common in India because of the caste system and cultural practices, although that is changing a bit now. But I wasn't really considering adoption—saying that was a way of softening what sounded to my friends like a harsh decision.

Even now when I go to India, my friends pressure me to have children. To them something is wrong with any woman who chooses not to. But on a recent visit I had an interesting exchange. I bumped into some old friends, a married couple. He is in his early fifties, she is forty-nine. In conversation they asked, "So how come you don't have children?" and I answered, "Oh, I chose not to." The man said, "What do you mean, you chose not to?" and I repeated, "I chose not to." The man said, "Wow . . . I don't know whether to admire you for that or think you're out of your mind." The woman simply said, "You're so lucky that you could make that choice."

Telling my Indian friends was a big part of coming to terms with my decision, making peace with it. Telling my parents was another milestone, and it was not easy. They came to visit after my ex-husband and I had been married for three years. Of course they had thought I would be having a child at any time.

When I told them I wasn't planning to have children, they couldn't believe it. My mother thought I had become too Westernized. She said, "You don't have to give up your career to have a child. I will move here and care for it." I think she said that out of hurt and disappointment, and I reassured her that my decision had nothing to do with my career.

My marriage ended amicably over a lifestyle question: my husband wanted to move to the country, and I wanted to remain in the city. When I told my parents we were divorcing over this, they had a very tough time with our decision. Divorce is shameful in traditional Indian culture, and women aren't supposed to show such independence. They kept pushing me to work things out, and my mother advised me to have a child. In India that is what many women do when there is trouble in a marriage, and I believe that's true in other cultures as well.

Most of my academic research is on women and land ownership in India. The Indian government has launched a program to give wasteland to poor women, and by farming, the women are able to make a livelihood. I'm studying what this means for the women's self-reliance, self-sufficiency, and power. A friend and I are documenting the sustainable community that the women are developing from scratch, and we are raising money for them so that in hard times they have something to fall back on.

I'm fortunate to be asked to do a lot of public speaking. I talk about issues that women in other countries face, with a focus on economics and the gap between rich and poor. When I was a girl I couldn't imagine that I would someday be trying to change the world, but my work is a big part of my life. It isn't just a job, it's what I am committed to, what I am meant to be doing.

I haven't planned my life, laid out my career or personal path step by step, but things have worked out pretty well. I would love to become a philanthropist, and in some ways I am already cultivating that in myself. For example, my will is a trust for women and children in India. One of the fastest-growing trades in Asian countries is the trafficking of children, especially girls, in the sex trade, and I would like to form a foundation to help these young women become economically self-sufficient by other means.

Not having children allows me more freedom and flexibility to travel for my research and also lets me volunteer more with organizations that serve women and children, neither of which I would be doing to this extent if I were tending children and supervising their schooling. I am also able to financially support five children and three village schools in India. Because of the choices I've made, I can contribute in a constructive way that is meaningful to me. The way I live supports what I believe in. I'm happy, and I love my life.

Martha Dorn, 38, grew up in Manhattan.
Her father was a pioneer in the computer industry,
developing data processing systems starting in the 1960s.
Her mother, who was a homemaker during Martha's early childhood,
became a public high school teacher and later a fund-raising and
development professional. Martha has an older brother.

Her first job was that of an editor and columnist for Savvy magazine.
She later worked as marketing manager for a men's professional
tennis association, an account executive for a public relations firm,
and a special-events fundraiser and administrator for
two national health organizations. Today Martha is director
of a four-day biking event that raises funds for AIDS education
and services. She has a bachelor's degree in sociology.

Martha lives with Ron, her husband of seven years, and their two dogs,
Barney and Sophie. She loves to garden, play bridge, and read mysteries.

MARTHA DORN

At the end of a long day of addressing many seemingly unsolvable

problems, I would think to myself, "What is it all about?"

And yet when I can get a group of farmers low-interest loans and

the right technology to improve their lives, I feel tremendously fulfilled.

The high point in life is being able to do something for your fellow man.

CORAZON AQUINO

MY PARENTS' PRIORITY WAS THAT THEIR KIDS
get some culture, so my brother and I spent our Saturday morn-
ings at the Metropolitan Museum of Art in a children's education group. We also went to young people's concerts conducted
by Leonard Bernstein, and I studied modern dance from age five
to fifteen. To me it was all enjoyable, and today I value that
background.

From the time I was young I knew I wanted to work. My mother
always did volunteer work and was very good about including me

in it. I remember being dragged to the League of Women Voters office and being deposited with the switchboard operator, Helen, who let me plug in the cords on the old PBX system.

Later Mom began doing fund-raising for Stanford, and when I was in second grade she started substitute-teaching, then went full-time so my parents could afford to send my brother and me to private schools. Mom taught reading to teenage boys who'd been thrown out of high school for offenses like beating up the elderly librarian or setting fire to the auditorium. When she reached the end of her rope with that, she became a professional fundraiser for an Ivy League university and a major art museum. Today she's vice president of a major hospital and vice provost of a medical school. I have always admired her career.

In college I was surrounded by friends who talked about getting out of school, getting married, and—boom—starting a family, and for some of them that's how it happened. I married when I was thirty-one, and they had written me off as the old maid! My friends who are parents love their kids but for years they have been up to their eyeballs in dirty diapers, and I believe they have moments of thinking, "Martha knew what she was doing." I never felt that I was supposed to get a great education and then marry and have babies and not use it. I wanted to work and live life and not have to go running home to the kids.

My first job out of college was at *Savvy*—"the magazine for executive women"—and I eventually became the editorial business manager. At *Savvy* the issue of having kids or not was a hot topic in the early and mid-eighties, and I was around people who had no problem with women not having children. I internalized that acceptance, and I also noticed the women in their forties who had gone back to work after their kids were born and who were struggling with the beginnings of the "supermom" syndrome.

During my early working years I was involved with one man whom I liked very much, and things would have gotten more serious with him if I'd wanted to have children. I was not yet saying "definitely no" to having kids but I was saying, "I'm not sure," and that in itself was scary to him. I suppose at the time it saddened me to realize that relationship wasn't going anywhere, but I felt strongly that I was a package deal and should not change who or what I was in order to satisfy someone else. As it turned out, not being interested in motherhood later gave me a certain dating freedom; unlike some of my friends, I wasn't concerned about finding a man whose children I wanted to bear and who could be a great provider.

In my late twenties I was recruited by a public relations firm to work on a promotion for the Summer '88 Olympics in Seoul, South Korea. The promotion took us twenty thousand miles around the U.S. in a recreational vehicle from April to September, when the Olympics began. That summer I met Ron, who had also been recruited for this promotion. We spent six months living in a twenty-two-foot Winnebago—we joke now that we skipped the dating part and went right into living together—and had a great time.

At the end of the summer I knew that I didn't want to work in public relations anymore and that Ron and I were in love. Six months later I quit my job, moved to be with him, and took a year off before going back to work. We married in a small ceremony with about fifty guests in my cousin's backyard.

When Ron and I were getting serious we talked about children, and he had no problem with my not wanting to have kids. On the contrary, it made me that much more attractive to him. He is eight years older than I, has an adult daughter from a previous relationship, and had a vasectomy when he was in his late twenties. Once we were engaged, I felt relieved and free because not wanting children was no longer an issue.

Ron is my Rock of Gibraltar and best friend. My work can be stressful, and he grounds me. Ron works from home and keeps the house going, buys groceries, takes my clothes to the dry cleaners. If we talk by phone when I'm at the office and he hears tension in my voice, he shows up at lunchtime with a picnic.

Ron isn't the man my parents had in mind for me; he's not Jewish, and he's not a doctor, lawyer, or stockbroker. Yet he innately knows me and loves me truly for who I am, and after seven years our marriage still has the romance that many people say goes away after a year. Two weeks before my father died, my family had a gathering that I couldn't attend because I was away on business. At that gathering Dad told one of my cousins that he realized I was happier than I'd ever been. I know he finally understood how much Ron contributes to my happiness.

I think it was difficult for Mom to accept that I didn't want to be a mother, but she's come to terms with my decision. Mothers expect to have something special with their daughter when the daughter goes through pregnancy and child rearing—that pick-up-the-phone moment of "Ma, the kid is throwing up! What should I do?"—and my mom will not have that with me. It helped that my brother, Charles, and his wife had kids—first twins, then a third child—and for all her ongoing dedication to her career, Mom is a doting grandmother.

It was also difficult for my grandmother, who passed away last year at age eighty-seven, to accept that I wouldn't be having children. She knew how attached Ron and I are to our dogs, and she used to say, "What a waste! All that love, wasted on dogs!" And I'd say, "Oh, Gramma, Gramma, Gramma . . . " When she got some great-grandchildren from my brother, the comments subsided.

Charles chose to go away to boarding school when I was in eighth grade, and after he finished college he moved from Manhattan, so we've never been close. But I adore his children, and they know where Auntie Martha and Uncle Ron live. We make a point of sending them really cool presents because that's what sticks in the minds of four-year-olds.

I have a vision for my relationship with these kids, and I know what it's based on. When I was thirteen Charles and I spent the summer with my Aunt Nadine and Uncle Mark in California, and they took us to Yosemite, Carmel, Monterey, and San Simeon. We couldn't get over the trees! I also spent my sixteenth summer with Aunt Nadine and Uncle Mark and grew close to their daughter, Lisa.

I love that my aunt wanted to show me that there were lifestyles other than the one I was living and places other than Manhattan. Thanks to her I saw that people can live in houses as well as apartments, know their neighbors by name, and live a mere hour's drive from tremendous natural wonders. Those summers had an impact on me, and I hope to have Charles's kids spend similar times with Ron and me so we can expose them to new ways and places too.

People who work for nonprofit organizations don't do it to get rich. I have a well-rounded fund-raising background, and my focus is special events, which take a lot of work. It's not nine-to-five work, either, as volunteer committee meetings are scheduled in the evenings and events are usually on weekends. It takes all my time and energy.

I've seen women in my profession who have children, but I don't know how I could do what I do and have kids at home. I've had employees who have gotten pregnant and had the first baby, then the second baby; aside from the fact that they're exhausted all the time, they also seem to have a cold year-round because kids bring germs home from daycare.

The number of women I know who work and whose kids live at daycare amazes me. You hear about supermoms who juggle career and motherhood, and I wonder how they have time to go to the bathroom. I don't see where they get quality time with their spouse or time alone, or how the kids benefit from the arrangement either.

Earlier in my career I worked for a health agency for which I raised more than eight million dollars, and in that time significant gains in medical research were made. I feel good knowing that my work can make a difference in people's lives. In my current job I have an opportunity to contribute to AIDS-related efforts, which is important to me because one of my best friends died from AIDS. That's a driving force behind my work today.

Thirty years from now, I hope not to be working but rather volunteering—I have too much energy not to be active. I'll play a role in the lives of my niece and nephews, who might by then have families of their own. I see myself doing a lot with Lisa and various friends. Even though we grew up far apart, I was always Lisa's "big sister," and today we see each other every week and talk constantly. I know we'll remain active in each other's lives.

Who would have thought that a kid who grew up in Manhattan would fall in love with gardening? I did, and it shocked me, but I've discovered weeding to be the most amazing stress-releaser. My grandmother was a phenomenal gardener, with roses her specialty, and I've embraced that. When Gramma passed away, I dug up a few of her rosebushes, which had been established for fifty years, and transplanted them in my garden, where they continue to bloom. I can see myself spending quite a bit of time in the garden when I'm old.

I imagine traveling more later in my life. Since my relationship with Ron began in an RV, our joke is that we will buy one someday and cruise around in it. I spent part of my junior year in college in London, I've been blessed with opportunities to travel around Europe, and I want to see other places as well. Ron doesn't have much desire to travel overseas, but we have the kind of relationship in which, if I make travel plans with a friend, he'll give me a ride to the airport, kiss me, and say, "Have a blast!"

Neesah Heart, 34, grew up on an Iowa farm.

Her father was a building maintenance manager,

her mother was a homemaker, and her family ran the farm.

She has two younger brothers.

Neesah attended college for two years,

then worked as a waitress, childcare giver, and peace activist.

For the last 10 years, she has been a licensed massage therapist.

She lives with Sandy, her partner of three years, and enjoys hiking,

being with friends, gardening, food, movies, and music.

NEESAH HEART

In the Native world view, there is no in or out;

everyone in the circle is necessary for the benefit of the whole family

of human beings and those that walk, crawl, swim, and fly.

DHYANI YWAHOO

WHEN I WAS ABOUT FOUR YEARS OLD I TOLD my mom I wanted to be a farmer. She said, "You can't be a farmer because you're a girl, and a farmer needs a wife." I stomped away, thinking, "So I'll get myself a wife!" Did I decide my sexuality based on needing a wife to be a farmer? I laugh at that now, but somehow I knew even then that saying I'd find a wife was not socially acceptable and certainly not acceptable to my parents.

As a teen I wanted to be completely different from my parents. I also wanted to "make it" in the world, so I planned to become a stockbroker and live in New York City. But in college I dabbled in women's studies. I visited the women's center on campus and became aware of environmental groups. This led to a decision to instead become a feminist therapist, but a year later I saw that reading books would not make me a therapist, and I decided to try my hand at life instead. So from childhood to college I held the images of being a farmer, a stockbroker, and a feminist therapist but never a mother.

My ancestors came to the U.S. from Poland. For seven or eight generations, all of them stayed in the community in which those first immigrants settled. My mother and father's generation moved thirty miles from the original community, and most of their siblings' families still live within that small geographic circle. I'm among the first to move farther away.

In my family everyone was given a limited future role: Marry your high school sweetheart, have kids, and live down the road. It confused my parents that I didn't do what they set out for me to do. Once I started stepping out of the box in my teens, they didn't know how to handle me, and by the time I was eighteen, I had left their planet. I think they hoped that some man would take pity on me and propose marriage. When I was still in contact with them, I did express once that I wasn't drawn to motherhood. Their response was quiet disapproval, the shaking of the head, no comment. And, as I saw it, there was a continued assumption that I would get married and have children.

I don't feel especially pioneering about not having children. People are abstaining from reproducing because of population concerns or because they recognize they don't have the emotional or financial resources to be parents. Others want a career. Some just never feel right about parenthood. To me, the decision's not that big a deal. But if I still lived in small-town Iowa it would be a *huge* deal. It would be the first thing out of my relatives' mouths every time they saw me. In the city where I live, I'm surrounded by people who don't care whether I have children. It's OK to be who I am.

The urge to be a mom has never lasted more than a few days for me—usually only a few hours and usually timed with interactions with small kids during those Kodak moments of "Oh, aren't they cute and soft, and don't they smell good?" If you hang around parents, you quickly see that being a mother is a twenty-four-hour-a-day job. I've pondered motherhood but I've never had a strong sense that I could do that twenty-four-hour-a-day job for twenty years. And I've come to realize that I have fears about what kind of parent I would be. I wouldn't want to repeat my parents' mistakes.

In other words, I've never heard a really strong "yes" about motherhood. And if I'm not getting a strong "yes" answer to a question I ask myself, I know that the answer, sometimes regrettably, is "no." The longer I sat with the "no" about having children, the more certain I felt about it. It's empowering to say "no" if you don't hear a "yes" because you can then ask yourself another question: "I have a certain amount of energy that isn't going to get taken up in this 'yes,' so what do I want to do with it?"

In my observations, children fill up a woman's life. If I had been trying in any way to avoid questions about who I am, what my gifts are, and how I will share those with the world, then a baby would have given me a twenty-year ticket out of that contemplation. Tending to children leaves little time for yourself, and most mothers don't get to do the amount of inner work that I've needed and wanted to do. The best part of not having kids, the part I'm happiest about, is that I can let the questions come and explore all the possible answers.

My involvement in women's spirituality has been one vehicle for that exploration. Women's spirituality contains a lot of goddess references, such as the phrase "maiden, mother, crone." Notice it's not "maiden, *woman*, crone"; it's *mother*. In this view of womanhood, you get to be a maiden just as you are, and a crone just as you are, but "mother" implies you've had sex with a man, become pregnant, and given birth to a baby. In this spiritual view you're supposed to create a human being. Some enlightened facilitators at women's spiritual gatherings open up the discussion to acknowledge the many ways of mothering in the world. But the nurturing of other adults, for example, is seldom mentioned as an aspect of mothering.

In addition to goddess spirituality, I've incorporated elements of Native American spirituality into my life. In Native spirituality, the physical risk of birthing is an initiation rite: going to the edge of life and death to bring another soul through. One of my questions is, How can I walk to the edge, risking everything, to bring something into this material world without birthing a child? Activities such as heading an organization or creating a painting seem small by comparison. I also wonder, How can I understand and connect to women past, present, and future without sharing the common denominators of childbirth and mothering?

I think the push to have a child — and the urge that women who are mothers may have to encourage other women to do it — is that we know it is deeply transforming. Our society offers no alternative for how to be so deeply transformed and valued and no similar ritual for bonding into the tribe of family and community. Even as advanced as our questionings are today, all our mythical stories feature mothers. If a goddess is childless, such as the Greek goddesses Athena and Artemis, that part of their psyches is not discussed. Archetypally, we haven't as a culture dealt with a woman's choice not to have children, and that failure results in a stigma for childless women.

I don't grieve not having children, but I do miss not having had those months of carrying a child and giving birth. I don't want the twenty years afterward, but the energy of pregnancy and birthing — it's the primal ritual, and for a ritual hog like me to miss it! But I'm compensated by my relief about not having to juggle one more thing on top of my daily to-do list of relationships, work, friends, house-keeping, and self-care, not to mention the relief I feel at not trying to be somebody I'm not. I feel joyous and grateful that I have a choice, that I'm free to take advantage of so much that life offers.

Some lesbians consider it a hardship, but I think one of the beauties of lesbian relationships is that women can't get pregnant with each other. They have to really want a child to go through trying to arrange a pregnancy. I wish heterosexuals had to make that con-scious of a choice to have kids. Perhaps becoming a parent should be like getting your driver's license: People should have to pass training before they're handed the keys to their reproductive sys-tem! And perhaps fewer of us need to be drivers. In my opinion the planet could do with at least a quarter fewer people. I don't think we're such a sacred species — that each one of us is *sooo* special — that we all absolutely have to be here on earth. I think we take ourselves too seriously and attach way too much importance to ourselves.

My mother and father blew it in their attempts to be parents, which is why I joke that you should need a license to have kids. My mother tried to commit suicide after I was born. She's told me she was ready to walk out of her marriage when she discovered that she was pregnant with me. She felt trapped, I assume, and stayed in the marriage. Her own mother had died when she was fourteen, and she had been left at home with a father who ruled by the strap. Certainly many of her fears and sadnesses must have been trig-gered by becoming a mother herself. I'm slightly older today than she was when she gave birth to me, and I sympathize with her story and feel sad for her. In many spiritual traditions you can send love and energy to someone's soul through time and space, and I do that with her young-mother image now.

Our society promotes a mythical view of The Family in which parents are automatically loving and devoted to a child. The myth is that anyone can have a child, and things will work out. But I have dealt with memories of incest, and statistics tell us that many kids are abused and neglected by their parents. I think there's nothing automatic about love, and nothing automatic about being able to provide adequate parenting.

I have many creations: massage, gardens, drawings, beadwork. In my massage therapy work I tend to stay in the same routine, possibly because it's effective and my clients say they love it. For me there's creativity in finding the flow of energy, and when I touch somebody I try to intuit how to proceed: Should I move fast or slowly? How long should I hold this body part? How can I move with the breath? The interaction is very subtle, and it can be perfect and glorious. Painters, no doubt, paint a lot of passable paintings that they sell to pay the rent. I give a number of passable massages that are good, and once in a while I give a masterpiece massage and think, "Wow!"

My contribution to the world will be of a feminine nature—that is, not necessarily lasting, like a monument or an organization, but more of-the-moment and earthy, like massage. I have leadership urges and strong opinions, and I don't know where these will take me; maybe I'll teach classes on healing and massage or become a naturopath someday. The older I get, the longer I give myself to find my authentic self because it was buried for so long and takes a while to unearth.

One of the nice parts of goddess spirituality is that women are valued for who they are, as they are, at every stage of their lives — especially in old age. The crones are the wildest group at women's gatherings! There, the old women are recognized as teachers, and menopause and wrinkles are respected. These women are role models for me, and they make me feel like I can't wait to get old. I'll welcome having friends of all ages, I'll be a part of wonderful circles, and hopefully I'll have figured out how to say my wisdom well and in a way that will reach and serve others.

Joy Michaud, 40, grew up in Wisconsin.
Her mother was a homemaker and her father sold real estate.
She has three brothers.

Joy earned a master of science degree with a specialty in
water resources. For more than 15 years, she has worked
as a water-quality specialist—for a state department of ecology,
consulting firms, the U.S. Fish and Wildlife Service,
and today in her own consulting business.

She has lived with her partner, Jack, for eight years and
with her dog, Jazzbo, for 14 years. Rock-climbing, mountaineering,
and backcountry skiing are among Joy's favorite activities.
She also plays volleyball, gardens, and enjoys reading mysteries.

JOY MICHAUD

We are here because there are things that need our help.

Like the planet. Like each other. Like animals.

The world is like a garden, and we are its protectors.

B.B. KING

MY FAMILY SPENT SUMMERS ON A LAKE IN A cottage that my grandfather built. My mom has a twin sister, and her family was always at the cabin when we were there. My brothers, my cousins, and I were a tribe of kids, wandering in the woods and having fun, living the good life. Today I couldn't imagine raising children any other way.

Growing up with brothers and in a neighborhood full of boys, I was a tomboy. When I became a teen I saw that what I continued to want to do with my time was quite different from what my friends in the all-girls high school I attended wanted to do with theirs. I felt like an oddball because I wasn't focused on having a steady boyfriend, as they all seemed to be; I dated but I was much more interested in riding my horse and going to ballet class.

This sense of being different has persisted in my life—being the only girl in a family of boys, the only Democrat in a family of Republicans, the only environmentalist, the only one who moved away from home, the only . . . the only . . . These days I'm quite comfortable, satisfied, and proud of who and what I am. If I'm an oddball, then that is exactly who I should be.

I was raised Catholic, and if those religious principles had "taken" with me, I'd be having children right now. I saw for the first time how religious training can influence people when I came home on a holiday break during my freshman year in college. A bunch of us high school friends got together to visit, and I ended up in a heated argument with them about their intent to have large families. These girls were from wealthy families and were attending expensive universities, where they would meet guys who were also wealthy and going to be successful. During this argument their point was, "If I can afford to have six kids, I should very well be able to have them."

Even then I was an ecologist, and I thought these friends displayed a total lack of awareness about the shape the world was in. My response to them was, "No way! Kids are not something that only the rich should have. Just because you can afford to have eight kids does not mean that you should. What about poor women? Do they not get to have *any*?" At one point during this argument I said, "I'm not going to have children at all," and they said, "You can't say that! If God gives you children, you take them." I was stunned at this reply, which seemed to come right out of the Ice Age. They were furious at me, and I was shocked at their philosophy. This incident was my introduction to the way much of the world thinks.

I never felt that I wanted or needed to have a child. For me, it wasn't so much deciding *not* to have children as it was an absence of deciding *to* have them. Having children should be a well-thought-out decision instead of a step that people take without thinking about alternatives or because they feel they've reached a time in their lives when it seems the thing to do.

Although I knew that I wasn't naturally driven to motherhood, I was told in my twenties that that would change. "When you hit thirty," people said to me, "a biological alarm clock will go off, and you'll want a child." Yet I felt no different at thirty. I was also told that when I hit forty, I would likely go through a period of great depression if I had not had children. This hasn't happened either.

Until now I've been working on my education and building my career, and I'm at a point where I have the money and independence to go on climbing trips, have adventures, travel, do all the things I love and value. For example, a few years ago I traveled in New Zealand with a close friend for a month, and if I had kids that would have been impossible. In other words, even at my relatively young age I can sit back a little and enjoy life. My mom once said she thought I was being selfish by not having kids, selfish for not wanting to give up my freedoms, and I've seen that people can have a bias against voluntarily childless women: they see us having too much fun and free time and not taking on enough responsibility.

It seems like society rates and values people in funny ways. Traditionally we have rated women according to how their kids turn out: Are their kids nice? Are they clean? Are they bright? If women don't have kids, people can't rate them at all but will instead assume that they are infertile, their relationship is troubled, or something else is wrong. An acquaintance recently asked me, "Why don't you and Jack get married and have kids? Then you could make plans for the future." To her, the "problem" is not just that we aren't having children but also that we're not married. I don't expect women my age to think that way anymore about marriage, but a lot of them do. And I was amazed that people could think we don't plan for the future because we don't have kids.

I've known women who have led lives similar to mine, who suddenly decide to have kids and become besotted with them. I understand that having kids totally changes things, and these friends now see motherhood as an indicator of how fulfilling their marriages and lives are. But I wish they could make the same assessment of my life as they do of their own, see that I'm happier than I have ever been, and understand why I wouldn't want to change a major element of my happiness.

I have wished that my parents could see that too. They communicate their disappointment about my not having children in various ways. For example, last summer when I was home, my mom and I were alone at the cottage, talking about the weather or something. Out of the blue she said, "I can't believe you're giving this up! You don't know what it means to me to be sitting here talking to my daughter and having you all to myself!" It was as though she wanted to say, "If I could only convince you, if I could say the right words, you would understand how important motherhood is, and you wouldn't give up this great opportunity."

I have felt moments of sadness in realizing that I won't have that strong link to my mother and to many women whose single, defining contribution was raising children. Nevertheless, that doesn't make motherhood the right choice for me, and in place of strong links to other mothers, I have strong links to many wonderful child-free women. My mom probably wonders if she did something wrong that resulted in her only daughter not having kids. She may think it reflects badly on her, and I wish that instead she felt it reflected well on her, that she felt good about raising a happy, independent thinker who has taken a less obvious path.

When I started out as a water-quality specialist, I was all ideals. I was going to lobby for major changes in environmental policy, influence people, make the world a better place. Then I saw how the business world and government agencies work and became discouraged. How would I make an impact? I kept a log that contained entries such as, "Saved fifty feet of stream by making developers put in a diffuser." That's what it came down to—convincing myself month to month that things were even a tiny bit better as a result of my work.

I stopped keeping that list, and I have lost a lot of enthusiasm for my field. I've talked to many people who feel that way about their jobs lately. Maybe it's part of getting older and wiser. But I stay in my profession because, as disappointing as it may be at times, I haven't identified something I want to do more that is likely to be any more beneficial. Also it doesn't make sense to turn my back on a going business concern.

Happily, in the last few years I've found a new outlet for my old enthusiasm. I've gotten involved as a volunteer in our local land trust, an organization whose goal is to preserve land that has high resource value, like stream corridors and wetlands. The people who own this land get a tax break while the trust protects the land for all time. Everyone wins. There's no conflict. It's really easy for me to get enthused about this! I give about a day a week to the trust and other volunteer organizations, and I walk away from our meetings feeling good about what I'm doing for the environment.

It scares me some to think about being old and not having any family around because I haven't procreated, yet it would be selfish to have kids for that reason. I do think that having children keeps you young because kids continually bring home new ideas, and that can expand your horizons. I expand my horizons by adding variety to what I read, taking classes, volunteering, and traveling. At this point I feel as though my life is expanding and the horizon is limitless. I guess the trick to not becoming stale and inflexible is to continue to learn and try new things and keep pushing that horizon back. That may actually be easier for women who don't have children to do, since sitting at home waiting for the kids to call or stop by will never be an option.

I've been with Jack for eight years, and he never wanted to have children—so much so that when we first got together, he asked how I felt about it. In his mind, if I had wanted to have children, there was no sense in our going on together. Luckily we both felt the same, and I didn't have to face the awful situation of falling in love with a man who desperately wanted to be a father.

When we met, Jack introduced me to rock-climbing, and I quickly became hooked. Rock-climbing is puzzle-solving with your body and mind in a vertical world. I can spend a day climbing and feel like I've been on vacation for two weeks. I've gone on climbing trips with women friends to Joshua Tree National Monument in California and Canyonlands National Park in Utah, and we talk of going to Italy to climb in the Dolomites. Recently Jack and I went to the north shore of Lake Superior and to the Black Hills of South Dakota to climb. There are all sorts of hidey-holes around the country that offer great climbing, and we love to explore those.

I expect that my women friends will be an even more important part of my life as I age, and I will probably rely on them as we grow old. Since Jack is older than I am, there's a fair chance I will outlive him, so I have joked with at least a couple of friends — especially my friend Jean, who is also an environmental scientist — about living together in our later years. Jean and I have laughed about what that will be like: We'll have pets — at least one dog, although she'll insist on a cat too — we'll raise some bees, poke around in the garden. We'll live in the country and be environmental activists. We'll be like the crazy ladies who currently drive us nuts at public hearings.

Ruby Burton, 84, grew up in a Utah mining camp.
Her father was an engineer and held second jobs as a deputy marshal
and truckdriver; her mother was a housewife. Her parents divorced
when Ruby was 16, and she and her mother moved to Los Angeles.
There her mother worked in a bakery and later in a factory,
and Ruby went to work as a "runner" in a court-reporting office and
eventually became manager. She is an only child and grew up
with 42 cousins, some of whom were like sisters and brothers to her.

Ruby was widowed in 1959. She and her husband had operated
a restaurant, and after his death Ruby went to court-reporting school
and worked as a court reporter for 20 years until her retirement.
Today she lives in a three-bedroom house where numerous relatives visit
regularly. She belongs to a book club and has logged 1,700 hours
as a hospital volunteer. Ruby loves reading science fiction and
is interested in mind-body medicine.

RUBY BURTON

You can live a lifetime and, at the end of it,
know more about other people than you know about yourself.

BERYL MARKHAM

I WAS A GREAT DAYDREAMER WHEN I WAS young, a talent fed by my early ability to read. From reading I developed a wide curiosity about what was going on in the world, and I wanted to get out there and see what it was like. If I had been born male I would have been all over this world. As it was, in my era women didn't have many opportunities, but I saw that at least I could refuse to be tied to the wheel with a husband and six kids. I love babies, and we had lots of them in the family, but I didn't see anything at all romantic about taking care of one. The feeding, the diaper changing—I had much more fun playing with a ball and bat.

A mining camp is a freewheeling place with all kinds of people. In the Utah camp where I was raised, the pressure was on to have kids, kids, kids. My Mormon girlfriends especially were following that route, and the more I saw that, the more I thought they were nuts—first get the husband and then have the kid, then another one, then another one, and never get an education, never get to go anywhere, never get to do anything, never find out who you are.

A friend of mine got married very young and lost any freedom to make choices because her husband ran the show. In our small town a husky high-school boy could get a job in the mines, make good wages, and think that made him a man. But most of those boys never went any further. One of my cousins married the town "catch," who ended up as superintendent of the mine. She had three children and died of cancer at age fifty-two. She used to go to Salt Lake City twice a year to buy summer and winter clothes, and that's about the only time she left town. I don't think they ever took a vacation.

My parents' divorce was the first in our family. In a small town in those days you had to have a man to support you unless you wanted to starve. After the divorce my mother moved us to Salt Lake City, then Los Angeles. I was sixteen, right at the age when you start dating, when you need a home and a father. I was hurt that my father could walk out on us, so easily shed his responsibility, and I was heartbroken to leave my seven aunts and uncles, grandmother and grandfather, and forty-two cousins. My mother and I hit Los Angeles in the bottom of the Depression, and I married when I was eighteen because I was lost. I was so damned unhappy that I just reached out to this guy who was cute and could dance well. It was my teenage error, and I finally got around to getting a divorce.

Even at that age I was amused by how some people regarded parenthood. When I was about twenty, into my office came this arrogant son of one of the partners in the business where I worked. He was engaged to a nice girl and proceeded to tell me that they were going to save themselves for marriage, and then as soon as possible they were going to have children because they felt they owed it to the world. I left the room because I knew I was going to burst out laughing. I think of that scene today when I see parents all puffed-up, looking at their children like "That's me!" Got to keep that magnificent gene pool rolling along, right? It may sound funny, but I think the number-one reason I wasn't interested in having kids is that I did not have the ego to want to clone myself.

I was twenty-three when I met Brandon, and it was love at first sight. But we were two independent spirits not wanting to be tied down, and four years passed before we realized we wanted to marry. He had a cockeyed sense of humor that I loved, and we had some crazy times.

Brandon and I didn't talk about having kids. We were busy running our restaurant and having a ball together. But the summer before Brandon was killed in a car accident, we had my cousin's twelve-year-old son with us. Brandon fell madly in love with this kid, and that brought on a surge of desire in him to be a father. He would leave the restaurant we owned, go home and get the boy, and then go out to the cattle auction, where he bought our restaurant meat on the hoof. The boy was with him every inch of the way, and when my cousin took his son back it broke Brandon's heart. He missed that boy for a year.

I have felt close to a few children myself. One of my cousins has a son I absolutely adore. I love his wife, too, and their three beautiful boys. I should treat all my relatives' kids equally, but I pick and choose because sometimes there's chemistry with particular ones. I love Mother's Day because I always get flowers and cards from my best friend's daughter and another cousin's daughter. I suppose you could say I have sort of mothered them over the years, helping to take care of their needs.

Today I'm helping to send one of my cousin's sons to college. He's a quiet, big, good-looking kid, working a couple of days at the mine and driving back and forth to school. Next year he's going to have to stay on campus, and whatever it takes, we'll get him up there. When I see someone who's trying like that, I want to help, and I can help because I'm financially secure. One of my cousins married a stock market genius who guided my investments. He was generous with me, so I can be generous with others.

My mother lived with Brandon and me until she died at age eighty. She kept house and cooked and washed, and she more than paid her way. For the last five years of her life, part of what I earned went to buy day help for her, plus doctors and whatnot. After she died I saved an appreciable amount of money and started investing.

When I retired at sixty-seven I thought I would go crazy. I had worked for fifty years, and I woke up every morning thinking, "Ohmigod, I'm late for work!" I had always loved my work—I was well paid, it was a constant challenge, and you never knew what was going to happen next in court. At first when I retired I didn't know what to do with myself, but then I began to volunteer with the hospital auxiliary, and I bought a plane ticket to Spain.

In the first ten years of my retirement I traveled to Spain, Portugal, England, Wales, Scotland, and Paris. Later I took three trips to the Orient, and I've been to the Caribbean Islands and through the Panama Canal twice. The most recent trip I took was with a friend who'd just lost her husband. We flew to New York and took the *QE2* to England, then took two train trips while we were there—one was to Paris through the Chunnel—and flew back to New York on the *Concorde*. We were spoiled rotten! I don't get around as well today as I used to but I still enjoy traveling with friends.

I don't think I'm kidding myself when I say that choosing not to have children was the right thing for me. I didn't see many women around me making that choice, but my gut feeling was that not having children was part of the road I was supposed to take. And so much that I saw over the years reinforced my gut feeling that I never regretted the decision.

I cannot imagine anything worse than being my age and regretting what you chose to do with your life because you don't have time to change things. Often it isn't what we have done that we regret; it is what we could have done and didn't do.

Nan Yurkanis, 45, was born in Minnesota.
Her father was a minister and the family moved frequently,
living in small towns and cities in Minnesota and Wisconsin.
Her mother worked as a teacher and professional weaver.
Nan has a younger brother.

After earning a bachelor's degree in education, Nan taught
third grade for a time and later did waitressing and office work.
After five years in an administrative support position at a university,
she resigned four years ago and began to study yoga.
Today she teaches eight yoga classes a week, including a "Women and
Menopause" class in an airy studio with a ballet bar and skylights.

Nan lives with Jonathan, her husband of seven years,
and Harmony, their cat. She is recovering from fibromyalgia,
a disorder that causes muscle pain and fatigue. She enjoys practicing
yoga, being outside, and spending time with friends.

NAN YURKANIS

Human beings are set apart from the animals.

We have a spiritual self, a physical self, and a consciousness.

Therefore we can make choices and are responsible for the choices we make.

ROSA PARKS

WHEN I WAS A GIRL I LOVED CHILDREN AND babies, and I wanted to be a teacher, the one in charge of them. My brother was born when I was seven, and I was thrilled with his arrival. I baby-sat him from the very start — I was much more confident caring for babies then than I am now.

A lot of my inclination towards motherhood when I was young was born of my desire not to disappoint my parents. They presumed I would have children, as most parents did at that time. And part of my later inclination not to bear children probably stems from my relationship with them too. They were both drinkers, and by the time I was eleven I was writing in my diary about my discomfort with my mother's drinking and my guilt at feeling that way.

Eventually her alcoholism led me to feel emotionally estranged from her.

When I was in my twenties and occasionally wondering about the prospect of having kids, I realized that I could have a child who for some reason might become as estranged from me as I had become from my mother. Today I don't feel that fear but I still understand its basis. The way I see it, how we have been parented profoundly affects our ability to parent. People who recognize that they grew up in a dysfunctional environment and who engage in a rigorous unlearning and retraining of their own parenting instincts can raise children effectively. Those who don't will likely do what was done to them in one form or another.

Many things about motherhood are not within our control; we don't know who we will become or what kind of child we might give birth to. I decided I wasn't a good candidate for the emotional risk-taking of parenthood. Today I still think that was a healthy reason not to have a child.

At heart I believe we're all "mothers," that men and women both do their share of mothering in the world. It's important for women who haven't had children to remember that we are still nurturers. We may not be changing diapers, but we assist children and other adults in various ways every day. Women ought to open up to one another concerning our choice about having children or not. We need to acknowledge that women who have children are not better or more credible than women who don't. I have certainly felt that bias more from women than from men.

Jonathan and I are lucky in that we are able to play a delightful role with our friends' children, whom we see often and look after occasionally. In addition to having friends whose kids are little, I also have a friend whose daughter is nineteen. This young woman and I had an instant connection with each other, and I hope we'll be friends for the rest of our lives. I cherish having friends of all ages, and the beauty for my young friend is that I'm not her mom or her aunt; I'm an older woman to whom she can relate differently than she relates to family.

I've been married three times. The first marriage, when I was twenty-one, lasted two years. I married again at twenty-five, and that marriage went through ten years of ups and downs due to drug use and emotional instability. We had a few pregnancy scares, and each time I felt very worried.

Getting high was such a focus in that marriage. We smoked pot every day, and I became addicted to sleeping pills as well as prescription drugs that I took for depression and anxiety. Yet we both held down full-time jobs and had a great deal of fun together: We camped, we went dancing regularly, and we were part of a tight circle of friends. We were nice, white-collar drug users.

Among other things, the drugs created a fog that made it hard to look at our marriage, and yet I knew our communication was poor and our relationship could never withstand the pressures of a child. I was sure that if he and I ever did have a baby together, I would end up as a single mother. We eventually realized we weren't interested in raising a child together, and he got a vasectomy, which was a relief to us both. We celebrated being free from birth-control worries.

When that marriage ended I quit using drugs. Two years later, when I was thirty-six, I dreamt that my life was going to include a very deep relationship. There was no child in that dream, which didn't mean that a child wouldn't possibly come out of this relationship, but I knew that the union itself was my heart's desire. The following year a friend introduced me to Jonathan, and for many reasons I felt he was the man I'd been shown in that dream. He told me almost immediately that he had had a vasectomy in his twenties, and something inside me relaxed completely. I knew that not having children was one hundred percent right for me.

Today Jonathan and I spend a lot of time together. We are NBA fans, and we love to go to movie matinees and for walks. We have an extraordinary friendship—there's such an ease, such a deep knowing of each other that goes beyond the number of years we've been together. We celebrate the good fortune of our partnership every day.

Just months after Jonathan and I married, I was diagnosed with fibromyalgia. I felt so intensely grateful for my decision not to have children, so clear why, whenever I had thought of motherhood, a voice inside me had always said "Wait." Maintaining my health is a full-time job. Each morning as I rise to begin my day with yoga and meditation, I'm grateful for the time to do these practices—time I wouldn't have if I had children to care for. My practices give me the energy to teach, which make them my most powerful act of service.

I perceive my role as a yoga teacher to be the role of student because I'm the one who learns the most. I used to say that when I taught third grade, and it's true in every yoga class today too. It also gives me joy to watch someone make a discovery about their own body or their own life as a result of working with yoga, which can be a powerful tool for change.

In class and on the retreats that I facilitate, I try to create a safe haven for people to explore their bodies' capabilities with no pressure or competition. I encourage them to toss out all critical thoughts—"I'm not limber enough, I'm too old, I'm too fat"—and substitute, "This is who I am today. This is where I start." People who know that I struggle with fibromyalgia are inspired to learn that I started practicing yoga seriously at age forty, willing to persevere and accept my limitations.

I've been asked how a woman like me, so involved with bodies—my own yoga practice, my struggles with fibromyalgia, my students' practices and their struggles with their bodies—can stand to miss the primary physical experience of pregnancy. My curiosity about the physical processes of pregnancy and childbirth has always been keen, but I can tell you that my dream world has given me all those experiences. I've had several dreams of being nine months pregnant, feeling the baby, giving birth. Those vivid visions have fully satisfied my curiosity. I know what it feels like. I've been there, on another plane.

I'm not interested in aiming toward retirement so I can get in a mobile home and drive around the country. I'd rather invest now in things that will sustain me over time. Jonathan and I talk about creating a yoga center, and maybe someday we will build another level on our house for a teaching studio. I also want to cultivate my artistic talents more: I love to sew, and I hope that in the future I will have a lot of time for that.

I expect to feel better and better as I age because my body is healing from a longtime disorder. People talk about going downhill physically, but for me things are looking up. In my old age I'll be vibrant with the kind of energy that people want to be near. I see myself limber, healthy, doing yoga every day. I see my needs as simple. I may be in a small house with a garden, hopefully with Jonathan, having tea with good friends, with a cat as part of the family.

Not raising children gives me the freedom to fully invest in my evolution, which is a great privilege and responsibility. My self-composed epitaph—"She loved being who she became"—sums it up perfectly for me, because I love being the person I am becoming. This is the life I have wished for.

Valda Thomas-Matson, 38, grew up in Seattle.
Her mother was an adult basic-education teacher and her father was
an American Baptist preacher. She is the eldest of four children,
two of whom died of sickle-cell anemia—a brother in infancy and
a sister at 25. She is the only person in her family
without the sickle-cell trait or disease.

Val holds a bachelor's degree in communications,
and she minored in early childhood development.
Formerly a television producer, she now works as a community organizer.
Val lives with Scott, her husband of three years.
Among the activities she enjoys are arts and crafts, long baths,
leisure hours with Scott, working on their house,
and entertaining friends and family.

VALDA THOMAS-MATSON

There is no duty we so much underrate as the duty of being happy.
By being happy we sow anonymous benefits upon the world.

ROBERT LOUIS STEVENSON

WHILE I WAS GROWING UP, MY PARENTS always seemed preoccupied with what they were "supposed" to be doing, like belonging to the PTA, going to church meetings, seeing that we kids were doing the right things. By all appearances, in our family the t's were crossed and the i's were dotted: we were polite kids answering the phone the right way, addressing elders with "yessir" and "nosir," always on time, keeping our word.

Those were good beliefs and behaviors, but to me the "joy meter" in our house registered low. I know today that my brother's death as an infant from sickle-cell disease and my sister's simultaneous showing of sickle-cell symptoms influenced our family life. But I also know that as a girl I wanted a fuller life than the one we were living.

I was a teenager when I realized that I didn't want to ever give birth. My family genes were riddled with disease—not just sickle-cell but also cancer, depression, glaucoma, high blood pressure—plus I thought I was ugly and no man would want to have children with me. So I didn't see myself married or bearing children but I thought I might like to adopt a child someday. When I understood this, I felt sad that I wouldn't experience one of life's most cele-brated ways of being a woman, and sad that maybe I wouldn't have "my own" to love and take care of me when I was old. But I also felt relieved and good about not passing along the bad genes that I thought were on the loose in my family.

During my late teens and early twenties, it became clear that I'd have to make my own way in life because marriage and children seemed so unlikely. If I were to be true to myself I'd have to create goals that could be meaningful to me, and I did. I decided that I wanted to go to college and buy a home by age thirty and adopt a child by age thirty-five or forty. Establishing these goals brought meaning to my life and boosted my self-esteem. I got busy being a well-adjusted and successful single black woman.

I dated a bit in my mid-to-late twenties, and it convinced me that I'd probably remain single. Dating during that time was like a pick-up basketball game, where you base a team on who is avail-able rather than on whom you'd like to play with. Some of the men I dated wanted to have a child with me. One had a daughter and wasn't pleased with how she'd turned out and wanted to try again. Another had four children and wanted one more!

In my early thirties I met two single women who had bought homes and adopted kids, and they became instant role models for me. I was proceeding on target with my vision when I bought my house several years ago, but then a wonderful detour appeared: I met Scott, and we married five years later.

On our first date Scott and I talked about children. I told him that I didn't see myself bearing kids but that I was thinking about adoption, and he felt fine with that. After we married we had occasional discussions about adopting, and usually they ended with, "Gee, will we or won't we?"

Today we don't see a need for it since we have so many children in our lives whom we love so deeply. I have what we in the black community call "play" nieces from my church; I read with one every other Sunday and do arts and crafts with the other. Scott and I are also guardians for two nieces, and we've made plans for another niece to spend the summer with us when she turns thirteen—I'm already excited and she's only ten!

Our friends drop their kids off at our house when they have evening meetings or need a break. Scott and I have books and toys for every age, and all the kids love coming to Auntie Val and Uncle Scott's house. Our society has lost touch with the idea of extended family, and I'm excited that Scott and I can play that role for several children.

Within the spiritual and cultural structure of our society, women and men have been told that a woman's duty is to reproduce and take care of the home and kids. That message was communicated loud and clear within my church when I was a girl. But I'm a creative rebel; I took full advantage of the positive spiritual aspects of the church and left the rest of the man-made rhetoric behind. As a minister's daughter I chose to find a way to stay in the church and make it fit who I am, and I've come away feeling good and true to my concept of God.

I had a "play" mother, Mother Hunter, who was my mother's age. I met her at church when I was twenty-five, and she loved me unconditionally. I could go to Mother Hunter with all my concerns and desires. Whatever I wanted to do, whoever I wanted to be, she encouraged me to go for it and helped me believe I could achieve it. Not many women are able to let their joy spill out wherever they are; with Mother Hunter's help I learned I could do that. I can't imagine her being disappointed by my decision not to have children.

It's a different story with my mom. Scott and I went to lunch with her not long ago and she asked, "So, am I going to be a grand-mother?" I said, "Well, you'll have to ask your other daughter because we won't be bearing any children." She was upset and said over and over, "What do you mean you're not having children? That's the reason people get married!"

My mother's disappointment hurt me. Yet I understand that Mom may have been looking forward to grandkids to help soothe the pain of losing two of her own children. Mom and I have differ-ent ways of seeing how life can be played out; she did what was expected of her, and I wanted to meet what I saw as fair expecta-tions yet also explore new ground.

I'm in a transitional time professionally, and I can feel my passion building for the next phase. For six years I've been a community organizer for the county, focusing on strategies for preventing drug and alcohol use by youth and promoting safe and drug-free neigh-borhoods. It's meaningful work, and I'm good at it and proud of my contribution. But I want to get back into television, specifically chil-dren's programming. I was cast to do a few small roles on the Disney-produced *Bill Nye, The Science Guy* show, and I carry a vision for myself as sort of a *Romper Room* character in children's programming. I've joined the board of directors of a local children's theater company, and that's also serving as a bridge to performing and production.

One of the things I am most attracted to in the world is other happy and intelligent black women. The oppression that black women have suffered and the way we've denied ourselves in order to nurture our children, our men, and our communities has left some of us without a capacity for joy for ourselves. As a child I didn't see a lot of black women having fun, and along the way I decided that my life would hold more of that. I make sure it does! For example, I arrange weekend getaways several times a year with three close women friends. We always go somewhere different, always on the water. We relax, cook terrific meals, and catch up on each other's lives. I expect that to continue.

I'm looking forward to midlife with Scott. I imagine it will be an intimate time for us, wholesome and cozy. We've grown so much in the seven years we've been together that I'm excited to see what twenty years will produce. He and I love to travel, and we usually take a month off in the summer to go somewhere. Before I met Scott I didn't travel much, and now I dream of going places I've never been—Australia, Europe, Africa. I see myself retiring early, freed up not only for travel but also for volunteering. At some point I want to help advance the research toward a cure for sickle-cell anemia, and I want to help children affected by sickle-cell, maybe in a summer camp setting.

I expect that when I'm old I'll still be kickin' it. I'll be a great storyteller, still evolving in my creativity and "gardeninghood"—yes, I'm gonna keep learning how to grow things, and I'll have it down by age seventy or so! When I was young I never had a hobby because I didn't feel competent, so that light is just starting to shine. It began with creative gift wrapping and rubber-stamping, and now I'm painting, cooking, and gardening, and there's so much more to explore.

I see myself in old age like the Delany sisters—alive, sassy, vital, exercising, taking vitamins, on target mentally, involved. I see Scott and me in our home, with young'uns—my nieces' and nephews' kids—running around, and us loving them and them loving us.

Maria Rodriguez is a 25-year-old Hispanic woman born and raised in southern California. Maria's parents were born in small towns in Mexico, immigrated to the United States as a young married couple, and became U.S. citizens. Devout Catholics, her mother is a housewife and her father a scientist, and they brought up their children in a middle-class suburb. Although Maria would be comfortable talking to her parents about her choice not to have children, she says that her parents' cultural upbringing, mores, and religious beliefs are so different from her own that she feels unable to talk freely about her lifestyle—her social activities, travels, and relationships with men.

Maria's story illustrates the difficulty that young women who are raised in traditional religions or cultures might experience in following their own paths yet remaining connected to their families or faiths. It also shows the frustration that they feel when their lack of interest in motherhood is disbelieved or mocked. Because I felt that including one such young voice could be relevant to young readers, I made an exception to my "real names" rule and permitted Maria to use a pseudonym.

MARIA RODRIGUEZ

When I look into the future, it's so bright it burns my eyes.

OPRAH WINFREY

IN MY EXTENDED FAMILY, CHILDREN WERE everywhere. As I was growing up, all my cousins had kids, and there seemed to be a new baby in the family constantly. To me it was gross that my cousins all got married young and had a baby nearly every year. I wondered, Why is their desire to procreate so great? How can they be so selfish as to not think about whether they're emotionally ready or can afford a child? How can they think that being bored, or wanting a greater sense of self-worth, or just thinking babies are cute is a good reason to create a life? I didn't see much thought behind their choices. It seemed that at a very young age they all began to say, "I want to get married, to get pregnant, to have a baby and take him to Disneyland."

My family has frequent get-togethers with our Mexican relatives, and I began to avoid these gatherings because I was constantly asked by my older Mexican cousins, "Who is your boyfriend? When are you getting married? When are you going to have a baby?" These questions started when I was fourteen! In Hispanic culture it's expected that young women will want to marry and become mothers, and in most parts of Mexico having children is primarily how women attain merit and status.

I couldn't relate to these cousins. They thought that my family and I were Americanized snobs, that we had betrayed them. But I wasn't betraying my culture, I just didn't agree with many aspects of it—in particular the aspect that dictated what women ought to do with their lives. Luckily my parents focused on their children's education, and there was never a question regarding my going to college.

Although she was raised in traditional Mexican culture, I believe my mom did not necessarily want to have children. In a conversation not long ago she told me that right before she met my dad she had enrolled in beauty school and was working at her first job at a shoe store. She told me how much she had liked her job and how fondly she remembered the ritual of going to work, feeling newly independent, and having a social life. I liked hearing that because I felt we finally had something in common, something that connected my urban American world with her small-town Mexican world, which she still often seems to miss.

My father has a definite double standard. On one hand, he believes women should behave modestly and socialize only in proper settings, but on the other hand he has never encouraged me to get married and be a submissive wife and have a lot of children. Although he was overprotective when I was growing up, today he encourages my independence, and when I've told him that I don't plan to marry, he says, "Good for you." Yet if he learned that I smoke, or that I have been intimate even once with a man, or that

I like to go out for a drink with friends after work, he would judge me terribly. In his view, that behavior is sluttish. And my mother would be nothing short of horrified.

I've been certain for a long time that I don't want to have children. I realize that a minority of women feel this way, but for me it was a natural choice, not monumental or profoundly emotional or hard to make. Although I enjoy older children and communicate well with them, I don't care for the company of little kids, and to me that's reason enough not to have any. People say to me, "Oh, it's different when they're yours," and I say, "Yeah, it's worse when they're yours because you can't leave them!" My natural disinclination to be a mother was reinforced when I got to college and realized that there is so much in life to see and know. I want to travel, write, dance, sing, and on and on, and that long list of passions doesn't leave room in my life for raising a child.

I've been involved in two serious romantic relationships so far. We were not casual lovers; we shared a deep bond and were responsible with and to each other, and that included using birth control. Today most of the men I date are in their twenties and seem to think of themselves as too young for parenthood, so my lack of interest in it doesn't affect who I choose to go out with. Later, though, it will.

I'm up front about not wanting kids, but maybe the guys who hear me mention it think to themselves, "You're too young to know your mind on this," or "You're just saying that now." I don't know if they fully believe me. When I'm older it'll be something that I'll say on the first date, because if a man wants children, I don't want us to waste our time on each other.

When the topic comes up and I tell friends or co-workers that

I don't plan on having children, they typically say, "Wait until you meet the right guy." That insults and frustrates me. I know that I don't want to become a mother, yet I've encountered so many people who question me on this point. It does no good to explain myself because they are not about to be convinced. So I'm honest and leave it at that.

As a teenager I didn't have much in common with girls around me who were going to parties and talking on the phone about boys. I loved school, and for me, doing homework, being tested, and competing with other students at the top of the class was exciting. My parents were strict about my going out, so I spent a lot of time in my room reading and listening to music.

Once I was on my own in college in Los Angeles, I got sidetracked by all the freedom. I lived in a dorm and could come home or not come home and no one cared! It was great, and everything else—including my education—went onto the back burner.

I like adventure and excitement, and after three years the distractions and temptations of L.A. proved too much. I temporarily lost the part of myself that loved learning, and all I wanted to do was have fun. I got into a Hollywood drinking-and-drug scene and became involved with a rock-and-roll musician who was addicted to speed. I saw the ugly side of life and it freaked me out. . . . Just as I broke up with him, a friend invited me to move to Boston with her. I knew I had to focus on my life again and I went. In that new place I settled down.

Today when I visit my parents in California, my mom and I are loving and affectionate with each other. We don't communicate about much outside of our family experience. I share only little bits about my life, because in my mother's traditional Mexican culture some of my activities are considered terrible; respectable women don't go out to clubs with their friends, so it's hard for me to tell her that I enjoy that kind of socializing, so common and acceptable in America.

My apartment is full of beautiful objects that inspire me. I love books, paintings, other types of art. I'm gradually replacing my favorite paperbacks with leather-bound and hardback editions.

I have so many passions that my mind is always debating, What am I going to delve into today? I appreciate the many facets of my personality that love to do so many different things, yet I still wonder how to create a whole life out of these individual parts. My priority right now is finding a new, challenging job that will offer me financial stability. Money is freedom, and it will underwrite the things I want to do: travel, take acting classes, learn to play the violin. I've had an offer to start a business with a friend and another opportunity to do TV commercials, and I'm free to pursue anything.

Recently I went to Europe for a month with a friend. Being there seemed so natural and normal. It was easy to walk alongside Europeans, doing what they did, eating what they ate, speaking their language. Maybe because I've read a lot about Europe and other parts of the world and because I've been exposed to different cultures, the world to me is not this impossibly huge place. It's very small and comfortable, and I think I will see much more of it in my lifetime. Writing and reading have afforded me the chance to know myself, which is key to knowing others, and traveling helps me see that people are the same all over the world. There are extremely different cultures, but human nature is human nature, and nothing is so different that we can't relate.

When I look into the future, I see myself with friends or family or with the means to hire somebody to take care of me. But I'm not in some house alone with my cats. I'm active until I can no longer pursue all the things I love. And I'll never, ever, get through the "list" of places I want to travel, books I want to read, art I want to appreciate.

I like to travel in a particular style, and it's not backpacking! I want to go back to Europe and dine on wonderful cuisine, dress fashionably, attend the opera and the ballet. I don't want to be in jeans, carrying a backpack like a tourist, standing outside the opera house and saying, "Wow, that must be cool in there. . . ." I want to be a guest, enjoying Europe as Europeans do.

I definitely don't want to wait until I retire to see the world, don't want to be barely making it out of the tour bus to see the Tower of Pisa. I want to travel while I can run up those stairs, see that view, climb that mountain, hear that music. And if I don't live to be eighty because I did crazy and wild things, then so be it. I'm not worried about living long; I'm worried about living well.

Mary Lambert, 36, grew up in Montana.
Her mother was a registered nurse and her father was a mechanic
at a factory. She is the youngest of seven children.

Mary attended college for one year, then went to cosmetology school
and has worked as a hairdresser for 16 years.
She counts walking, rollerblading, kayaking, and tennis among
her favorite activities. A self-described thrill seeker,
Mary has bungee jumped, sky dived, and flown in a stunt plane.
She lives with her boyfriend, Steve, and a dog and three cats:
Jazz, Myling, Frazier, and Elliott. Steve's daughter,
Sarah, lives with them every other week.

Because her job involves social interaction,
Mary's home life is quiet by design. She gets together frequently with
a few close girlfriends and one of her sisters.

MARY LAMBERT

Just trust yourself, then you will know how to live.

JOHANN WOLFGANG VON GOETHE

WHEN I WAS YOUNG I WANTED TO BE A NURSE like my mother because the helping part of her job looked fun. At home we had an old wheelchair, and my brothers and sisters and I used to wrap each other up in bandages and wheel each other around. By the time I was a teen, I had left the nursing idea behind, and after high school I decided to go to cosmetology school. Today, even after doing it for fifteen years, I continue to love being a hairdresser because I get to be creative. In hair design you look at the head, the line, the shape of the face, the type of hair. Every client's needs and wants are different, so the challenge is to see what I can come up with that will make them say, "I love it!"

Within my family I had different examples for my decision about whether and when to have children. Two of my sisters didn't plan on having kids, then changed their minds at age thirty-five; another sister who had had two kids by thirty-five had her tubes tied at that age.

Though the image changed when I got to know myself better, for a long time I assumed I'd have kids, for a few reasons. One, since I grew up in a large family, I imagined always living in a big family. Two, I like kids, and I'm a terrific aunt. And three, in our society the message to women is, "This is what you're built for, this is what you're supposed to do." Like most females, I'd grown up believing that message, and I've seen how that cultural conditioning plays out in my life.

For example, I was amused by my own reactions in discussions Steve and I had early in our relationship. When we first got together five years ago, I thought, "Wow, I'm going out with someone who has a child. This is going to be different from any dating I've done before." I remember asking Steve whether he imagined having more children, and he said, "No, I already have trouble keeping up with the one I have." At first I was angry at his response because I felt he was rejecting me. Then I thought, What am I mad about? I don't want to have children anyway!

I laughed at myself over that, wondering why I'd gotten uptight. But I understood that we all grow up hearing that if two people are really in love, they will mate and produce a child. They will prove their love to the world in this way. You have to throw that notion out to see that people can love each other deeply without wanting to create a child together.

Today Steve's seven-year-old daughter, Sarah, lives every other week with us. When we were dating and lived fifty miles apart, Sarah was little and I saw her only every other weekend, and our relationship was up and down. I'd walk in the door and she'd say, "Let's go play in my bedroom!" and I'd think, "I didn't come here to play dolls. . . ." But I slowly learned to say, "I'm going to talk to your dad for a while, then I'll come play with you for a little bit."

As time went on the three of us did more and more together, and Steve and I tried to incorporate kid stuff into our adult activities, like Sarah's riding her bike with us as we rollerbladed. At the beginning she was upset by my being her dad's girlfriend because she understood her dad and I might get married someday, which probably shattered any hope she had for her mom and dad reuniting. I understood her fears and was patient, and as she has gotten older, things have gotten easier.

I moved in with Steve and Sarah about three months ago. Because I have a long commute I see Sarah for only a short time before she goes to school in the morning and to bed at night, and we occasionally spend time together on my days off. I think that works for us because she still has plenty of time alone with her dad and I'm not expected to participate in "mom" activities like making meals or bath time.

Living with Steve and Sarah has affirmed for me that I don't want to have kids of my own. I never feel like or see myself as a mother figure to Sarah because she has a mother. Rather, I see myself as an important adult in her life, a grownup she can talk to or just be silly with.

There was never a time when the "light" came on and I knew I didn't want to have children—it just seems like the natural thing for me. But I can point to two events that confirmed it for me. The first happened about seven years ago when I visited a friend who'd just had a baby. Until then, whenever I'd be in a store with friends and they'd see a woman with a baby, they'd coo and say, "Oh, what a cute baby! I want a baby!" and my response was always, "Huh?"

But visiting this friend with her newborn, I found myself feeling for the first time a strong urge to have a baby of my own. I thought, "Ohmigod, I haven't done this yet."

But after only a one-hour visit I started thinking, "Ohmigod, I don't want to do this." The feeling of not wanting a baby was just as strong as the earlier feeling of wanting one. In that hour the baby had just lain there like babies do, but the baby was our only focus, and I saw that my friend had been transformed into somebody else. She could talk only about the child and was no longer interesting to be with. The memory of that moment is still fresh because it was the first time I had thought I wanted a child, and it was remarkable how quickly the thought passed.

The second realization came five years ago. At that time I said to my pregnant sister, "Maybe you should save those baby clothes for me because I might want to have a baby sometime." A month later I watched her in labor and delivery, and I said to myself and others, "I will never go through that." Her labor was awful, and she ended up having a C-section. It was horrible to watch her. I cried at every contraction.

After the surgery I called my family and told them of the birth ordeal. Later my mother said to my sister, "Well, that left quite the impression on Mary." To this day I've never had one moment of thinking, "Ooooh, I wanna have a baby." After the delivery-room experience, I knew definitely that I did not want to bear children.

One day not long ago my mom and sister and I were shopping, and my sister was looking at these little baby shoes. My sister remarked that one of our nieces should have a baby so we could all buy cute little shoes for it. And my mom said, "Maybe Mary should have a baby!" All three of us burst out laughing—that's the first time my mom ever said anything about me not having kids, and we all understood that it was fine to joke about it.

I have two nieces and four nephews who range in age from five to twenty-three. I baby-sat the older ones every summer when they were little. We did a lot of fun stuff together then, and we have even more fun together now as adults. My nieces and nephews tell me I'm their favorite aunt, and that may be because I do things with them that other adults don't. Once I took my twelve-year-old nephew and fifteen-year-old niece out and let them drive my car on some back roads. And for Christmas a few years ago I got a young nephew six cans of Silly Spray as a gift; when he opened them and came after me with the spray, I pulled out the can I had hidden in my pants and covered him with the foamy stuff!

Even though there are many light moments among us, my family has essentially been in crisis since my sister Beth was diagnosed with cancer a few years ago. Just before her diagnosis, all my sisters and I were sitting around one day with my mom, talking about some old feud Mom had with her sisters back in the 1940s. For Mom, this old quarrel still seemed fresh, and my sisters and I were laughing, saying that when we were seventy years old we weren't going to be feuding—we were going to be on cruise ships, traveling in Mexico, having all sorts of experiences together. The next week, Beth's life was put on hold.

Beth's cancer progressed fast. My mom, who is in her seventies, cared for Beth at Beth's home, and the rest of us all pitched in, taking turns being with Beth, giving my mom a break, helping to communicate good news or bad to the others. I was the one sent to talk to Beth's teenagers, Kim and Jason. I'm the one they listen to and believe, the one who could say to them, "OK, this is what's going on with your mom, this is what you've got to do." When Beth's condition worsened, the family made out her will together.

My family is close, but Beth's death a year ago pulled us even tighter together. We all know that we will care for each other in future similar situations. I've seen a lot of personal growth in all of us as we have gone through this loss. It's made me a better person, and I hope someday to help others who are facing the death of a sibling or parent.

Recently Kim, Mom, and I vacationed in Mexico. Although Kim and I behave like friends, being with her on that trip reinforced my sense of my role as her aunt. Young women in their twenties need their moms, and Kim doesn't have hers. I'm helping her in every way I can—listening, asking questions, offering advice. I talk on the phone at length with both Kim and Jason at least once a week, and we're close.

I see myself in my old age with my nieces and nephews. My aunt role may look more like a grandma role then, because I'll be an aunt not only to them but to their children too. I will always have my own life, and I will be connected to my family forever.

Louise Ross, 38, grew up in Korumburra, Australia, a small town near Melbourne. Her father is a retired lawyer and her mother worked as a fashion designer before becoming a full-time homemaker. Louise has one older sister as well as two older stepsisters from her father's first marriage.

After high school Louise trained to be a chef and used that training to travel and work throughout the United States, England, and France. She moved to the United States to earn a master's degree in Jungian psychology and counseling, later working as a counselor. Most recently, Louise has organized an open-air market for artists and craftspeople and has written travel articles for newspapers.

Louise loves to travel, golf, and downhill ski, and enjoys gardening, gourmet meals, and quiet time alone. She lives with Scott, her husband of nine years, in an apartment dotted with their original art.

LOUISE ROSS

To know what you prefer instead of humbly saying Amen
to what the world tells you you ought to prefer
is to have kept your soul alive.

ROBERT LOUIS STEVENSON

WHEN I WAS YOUNG, MY MOM OFTEN TALKED
to my sister and me about what would happen when we grew
up, and the talks never held any sense of choices. I believe this
reflected how my mom felt about her life. She described her own
story as, "I met your father and gave up my career when we
decided to move to the country and have a family." My mother
is creative and talented, and I believe that she carried regrets
about abandoning her career. She channeled her energies into
her family and maintaining a lovely home, she said, largely
because my father didn't want her to work.

The story Mum told my sister and me went like this: It is
important for you to get an education and have a career so that

when you marry and have children, you will always have something to fall back on if your marriage fails and you need to support your children. My sister swallowed the story hook, line, and sinker, and indeed her life unfolded the way Mum said it would. She divorced and was devastated when she had to return to work to support her child. She had wanted to repeat our parents' situation.

It's been quite different for me. Adults used to observe my sister, who loved to play with dolls and babies, and comment that she was going to be a great mum one day. But nobody said that about me because I never showed much interest in that kind of play. Very early I felt this difference between my sister and me, which transferred to feeling different from Mum, my aunts, my grandmother, and other girls my age who talked about one day wanting to have children. Feeling different didn't bother me; it just was—and still is—a part of who I am, and I'm comfortable with who I am.

I've always heard an inner voice that seems to be wise and old, and it propels me through my life. When I entertain ideas that aren't part of what I believe is my karmic direction, it says, "Uh-uh. That's not the way you're going." For example, my first serious boyfriend used to say he wanted a large family, and I can remember the voice was audible even then, saying, "No, no, you don't want six children. This is not the person for you."

I was pursuing my master's degree in the U.S. when I met Scott. After our first date I told my roommate, "I've met the man I'm going to marry." Our relationship began with an instantaneous, soulful connection, and he and I both felt we were meant to be. Scott doesn't make decisions fast, but he felt as compelled as I did about our romance, and we married a month after we met.

When Scott and I talked about getting married, I said, "You know, I don't want children." It was the first time I'd voiced my choice with certainty and conviction, and I was afraid to say it, knowing that Scott loved children and wanted his own. I wondered if his love for me was greater than his desire to be a father, and I suspected that if it wasn't, he would break off the relationship. If Scott had ended it, I would have been heartbroken but at the same time understood that we weren't meant to be together.

My psychology degree program required all students to undergo therapy, so I invited Scott to come into therapy with me to talk about our differences regarding wanting children. The therapist was a mother herself and encouraged me to at least entertain the idea of having a child. That, of course, really excited Scott. We left therapy, and for the first time in my life, at around age thirty, I shifted gears and began to think about what it might be like to be a mum. Scott and I looked at little babies and gaagaa'd. We played with friends' kids and made them giggle. In doing so I found out something about myself: I love children, especially little girls. But I also discovered something specific: I love small children for short periods of time, then I'm ready to give them back to their parents.

"When are you going to have children?" people asked me after I was married. My response through my mid-thirties was, "Maybe someday. I've got ten more years." I've always been careful how I respond to women's questions about when I'm going to have children because I fear being judged about this. So when a co-worker who had just become a mother asked me about when I'd have kids, I said, "Well, I'm not sure I'll have any." She replied, "When you really know who you are and where you're going, you'll have children." This annoyed me because it made me realize that women who choose not to have children can be perceived as aimless, lost souls.

I had a similar experience with an English friend who married a wealthy fellow. Before she married she asked me if I wanted children. I confided that I didn't think so, and she said she seriously questioned whether she did either. Well, after she married she did have two children—and a housekeeper and a nanny, all very British—and when I next saw her, she said to me, "Once you're more settled and in your own home, you'll feel ready to have kids." Although I wanted to, it didn't seem appropriate to say to her, "I don't think you understand—neither a house nor money would compel me to become a mum. I simply don't want to raise children."

To me these situations illustrate how women can be their own worst enemies, how cruel we can be in the way we judge and condemn each other for the choices we make. Exchanges like these still occur in my life, and I don't make a public issue of my choice or get into intellectual discussions about it because my friends are important to me and I don't want to create tension.

I think women often decide to have children unconsciously, and women who consciously decide not to have children challenge mothers to think about what they're doing, what they've done, and why. When your ideas about what you believe in are challenged, it's normal to get defensive. So I'm careful.

In graduate school I got a job as a counselor at a women's health clinic, and for three years I immersed myself in the drama of women deciding whether to terminate crisis pregnancies. I discovered that I couldn't successfully distance myself from the turmoil the women were in, and I had to admit that I was not cut out for one-on-one counseling.

After leaving the clinic, I wrote about the experience of working there but had no success getting my stories published. While writing, I found that I had to balance that cerebral activity with something physical, something hands-on and creative. Scott made me some furniture, and I decorated the pieces with decoupage, then started combining painting and decoupage to create large collages. Soon we began to feel confident about these items we were creating for our apartment.

Meanwhile, Scott had begun to sculpt, and I thought I'd try to get our work into galleries. When I learned that galleries take nearly half off the top in commission when an item sells, I wished for a market where we could sell our artwork ourselves. So I developed a proposal for an outdoor art and craft market and presented it to the city council; they approved it, and I spent about a year organizing the market. It expanded to include food, music, and entertainment and has become successful from the standpoints of both the artists and the community. Coordinating it has been so all-consuming that Scott and I haven't even displayed our own work!

I love projects like the market that allow me to generate ideas, be a leader, be community-minded, and energize people by helping them believe in the worth of what they do. I love to devote myself to projects ardently for a year or two—they become my babies—then usually I have a new idea and must move on.

I'm a late bloomer, and late bloomers learn to trust that things will be revealed as they go along. My life has taken a series of interesting turns, so I'm not a master of a particular job so much as I'm a master of change, with an accumulated cross section of information and skills.

Being late bloomers allows Scott and me to explore opportunities, and in that way our lives are different from the lives of our friends who have mortgages and children and must hold certain kinds of jobs to pay for both. I still feel like the world's my oyster, and I imagine it's easier for me to invite change into my present life than it would be if I had children.

Today Scott is channeling his creative energies into his design and artwork. His lifelong dream was to be an artist, and now he says to me proudly, "Be careful what you wish for!" Proudly, because he made his dream happen. The very first piece he sculpted was so beautiful, his teacher wanted to buy it. He began to work in steel, and his creativity just took off. Since I began organizing the art and craft market, he's become successful on his own through galleries and commissions. He's focused and prolific, and his art makes him very happy.

The whole creative process is so important to people who aren't parents because we need to channel our creative energy some-where. Scott's goes into his art and design, and my mine goes into projects like the market and writing. Scott's supportive of the work I do, telling me how proud he is of my determination to turn my dream projects into reality, and he also relies on my creative input and encouragement of his design work. There's this constant see-saw where I get feedback and support from him, then he looks for it from me. We are each other's Muse.

I imagine myself becoming more a teacher as I get older. I'm par-ticularly interested in being a role model for young women. Already I find younger women are drawn to me; they like to talk to me and tell me their secrets and dreams, and I love to listen and encourage them to follow their bliss. I've come to see that nurturing one or two children isn't enough for me, that I need to encompass a larger scope of nurturing. Perhaps one day I'll have a formal opportunity to nurture young women along their paths by speaking publicly to groups about the choices available to women today.

I went to boarding school, and that community-living experi-ence prepared me to live out my days in a retirement community where I have a separate unit joined to a shared living area. If Scott's not around at that point, then I'll spend time with other people — I'll go next door to my neighbors, and if they don't want company

I'll join whoever's in the common space. Today these communities have such wonderful organized activities—trips to the theater and out to eat, or people coming in to teach yoga and such. In boarding schools and retirement communities you're always surrounded by pals yet you can find space when you need it.

I will always need that private space. I'm not a person who has music or TV on all the time at home; I like to just sit and hear my environment. The quiet reenergizes my spirit and helps me dream, and dreaming is how I get a sense of where I'm going and what still needs to be done.

ACKNOWLEDGMENTS

I'M DEEPLY GRATEFUL TO THE 25 WOMEN whose stories appear in this book as well as those whose stories I could not include but which informed and influenced its spirit. Through their intelligent and candid sharing, I obtained more insight into my own story and began to more deeply examine my attitudes and outlook on life. Among these women I found superb role models for growing older.

I'm ever grateful to my husband, Dave Hussey, a steady provider of humor, perspective, love, and support. For "Otherhood" (my working title for the project) and for all the listening, feedback, and solid suggestions he offered during my work on this book, my deepest love and appreciation.

Cindy Black, editor-in-chief of Beyond Words Publishing, is an author's dream come true. In giving birth to books instead of babies, Cindy takes a collaborative approach to publishing titles that help people live authentic lives, and she shares her knowledge and experience freely. I'm happy we found each other. My appreciation also to Richard Cohn, Kathy Matthews, and the staff at Beyond Words, as well as to designer Susan Shankin and to my agent Sheryl Fullerton for their work and support.

I try to keep a daily journal in which I record, among other things, what I'm grateful for. Several dates from 1997–98 contain the same entry: Phyllis Hatfield. An extraordinary editor in Seattle, Phyllis was a mentor to me, and her advice and editing at every stage of this book is reflected in its pages.

First-time authors ask a lot of their close family members and friends, including endless small shows of enthusiasm and encouragement. I received such support across the board, especially from my sister Jeanne Porter and my friends Beth Eisenhood, Jan McCowan Box, and Jani Gilbert.

Thanks to Pat Lunneborg for her early optimism and advice, and to Nan Yurkanis, Jonathan Yurkanis, Leila Anasazi, Louise Ross, Maggie Lindley, and Monica Harrington for their critiques, ideas, and help in sorting through the questions.

Many others helped the project along in ways too numerous to mention: Gigi Anders, Freda Atkinson, Bee Bender, Mary Burki, Susan Codega, Ruby Dacia, Traci Drake, Diane Erdman, Laura Esther, Diane Evergreen, Rebecca Green, Rochelle Holt, Jean Jacoby, Sandra E. Jones, Beverly Kim, Dr. Susan Lambert, Karen Laurie, Joyce Manson, Julie Paschkis, Ruth-Ellen Perlman, Dale Peters, Irene Peters, Marilyn Strong, Katherine Sylvan, Mary Jo Torgeson, Peggy Walsh, Ruth Ward, Kim Williams-Brinck, Yvonne Zaske, and Karen Zaugg.

Finally, thanks to all the women over time who listened to their inner voices, made unconventional choices, and paved the way for the freedoms we experience today.

RESOURCES

MANY OF THE BOOKS, MAGAZINE ARTICLES, organizations, and Internet Web sites and chat groups that I have consulted might be helpful to you, so here is a list of resources that will offer information and a sense of today's discussion on choosing not to have children. Be forewarned: This is a miscellaneous collection, with a sometimes strange mix of attitudes and points of view—from tolerant and inspirational to petty and child-hating—and you'll have to sift through it to find material that appeals to you.

BOOKS

Because I think it's useful to hear several approaches on how women come to the decision not to have children, I list here a miscellany of books on the subject. Again, the authors' sentiments range from ambivalent to exultant and everything in between. These books were published since 1991, and you should be able to find them through your neighborhood bookstore or an online bookseller.

Bartlett, Jane. *Will You Be Mother? Women Who Choose to Say No.* London: Virago, 1994; and New York: New York University Press, 1995.

Cameron, Jan. *Without Issue*. New Zealand: Canterbury University Press, 1997.

Dyson, Sue. *The Option of Parenthood*. London: Sheldon Press, 1993.

Engel, Beverly. *The Parenthood Decision: Discovering Whether You Are Ready and Willing to Become a Parent*. New York: Doubleday Books, 1998.

Lafayette, Leslie. *Why Don't You Have Kids? Living a Full Life Without Parenthood*. New York: Kensington Books, 1995.

Lang, Susan S. *Women Without Children: The Reasons, the Rewards, the Regrets*. New York: Pharos Books, 1991.

Lisle, Laurie. *Without Child: Challenging the Stigma of Childlessness*. New York: Ballantine Books, 1996.

May, Elaine Tyler. *Barren in the Promised Land: Americans and the Pursuit of Happiness*. New York: Basic Books, 1995.

Morell, Carolyn. *Unwomanly Conduct: The Challenges of Intentional Childlessness*. New York: Routledge, 1994.

Reti, Irene, ed. *Childless by Choice: A Feminist Anthology*. Santa Cruz, Calif.: HerBooks, 1992.

Safer, Jeanne. *Beyond Motherhood: Choosing a Life Without Children*. New York: Pocket Books, 1996.

Ziman Tobin, Phyllis O., with Barbara Aria. *Motherhood Optional: A Psychological Journey*. Northvale, N.J., and London: Jason Aronson, Inc., 1998.

ARTICLES

Since magazine articles from even a few years ago can be hard to find, I have listed here only those that appeared in U.S. publications between 1996 and early 1998. Search for these at your local library or in the publishers' online archives. For other magazine and journal articles, see the bibliographies of the books listed above.

"Childless by Choice," by Jill Hamburg, *Working Woman*, March 1998.

"Couples in Pre-Kid, No-Kid Marriages Happiest," *USA Today*, August 12, 1997.

"Childfree by Choice," by Sherri Dalphonse, *Washingtonian*, February 1997.

"Childless by Choice," by Ann Wicker, *L.A. Reader*, May 31, 1996.

"Many Childless Couples Say They're Not Only Content, but Joyous," by Linda Murray, *Longevity*, April 1996.

"Childless by Choice: Can a Woman Be Happy Without Kids?" by Katherine Griffen, *Health*, March/April 1996.

ORGANIZATIONS AND WEB SITES

Nearly every organization for childfree singles and couples has an Internet Web site and also offers booklets, bulletins, or newsletters to anyone who's interested. Here is a list of them, with contact information.

The ChildFree Association provides support and information for both those who have chosen to not have children and those who are undecided and want more information. The association offers a subscription newsletter, a Web site with links to other sites of interest, and a message board for interacting with others who visit the site. The ChildFree Association, 1971 W. Lumsden Road, Suite 186, Brandon, FL 33511; e-mail: newtech@childfree.com; URL: http://www.childfree.com

No Kidding! is a nonprofit social club for couples and singles who, for whatever reason, are not parents. No Kidding! has chapters all over the U.S. and Canada. No Kidding!, Box 27001, Vancouver, BC, Canada V5R 6A8, (604) 538-7736; URL: http://mypage.direct.ca/d/dsimmer/nokids.html

British Organisation of Non-Parents (BON) is a support group for people who have chosen, adjusted to, or support being child-free. Its membership is evenly split between women and men and also between single people and couples. British Organisation of Non-Parents, BM Box 5866, London, England WC1 3XX

Childless by Choice is an information clearinghouse for people who have decided not to have children and for those who are deciding whether or not to become parents. CBC materials provide support, humor, and social commentary for and about childless or childfree people. Childless by Choice, P.O. Box 695, Leavenworth, WA 98826; URL: http://www.now2000.com/cbc/

The Childfree-by-Choice Pages
A clearinghouse of childfree information on the Web.
URL: http://www.childfree.net/contents.html

Childfree is a personal Web page that contains information and support for people who have chosen or are considering a childfree life. URL: http://www.missouri.edu/~c489011/

Planned Parenthood
810 Seventh Ave.
New York, NY 10019
Phone: (800) 829-7732 or (212) 541-7800
URL: http://www.plannedparenthood.org

Zero Population Growth
1400 16th St., NW, Suite 320
Washington, DC 20036
Phone: (800) 767-1956 or (202) 332-2200
Fax: (202) 332-2302
E-mail: info@zpg.org
URL: http://www.zpg.org

BEYOND WORDS PUBLISHING, INC.

OUR CORPORATE MISSION:

Inspire to Integrity

OUR DECLARED VALUES:

We give to all of life as life has given us.

We honor all relationships.

Trust and stewardship are integral to fulfilling dreams.

Collaboration is essential to create miracles.

Creativity and aesthetics nourish the soul.

Unlimited thinking is fundamental.

Living your passion is vital.

Joy and humor open our hearts to growth.

It is important to remind ourselves of love.